Funny Convulsing
and Funny Confusing

Also by Denys Parsons in Pan Books

Funny Ha Ha and Funny Peculiar
Funny Ho Ho and Funny Fantastic
Funny Amusing and Funny Amazing
Funny Funny Funny

Denys Parsons

FUNNY CONVULSING AND FUNNY CONFUSING

A Pan Original
Pan Books London and Sydney

First published 1971 by Pan Books Ltd,
Cavaye Place, London SW10 9PG
3rd printing 1976
© Denys Parsons 1971
ISBN 0 330 02726 3
Printed and bound in Great Britain by
Cox & Wyman Ltd, London, Reading and Fakenham

INTRODUCTION

I never thought the day would come when people would be using Gobfrey Shrdlu's exploits as a kind of barometer for day-to-day living. Yet I recently received this heartening letter signed 'Constant reader':

I am approaching my 80th birthday. I keep your books at the bedside. Every evening I mark off three items for reading immediately on waking next morning. If I get three laughs I know I am in for a completely good day; two laughs, not so complete; one laugh – go with caution; no laughs – I take a dose of salts.

For new readers, Gobfrey Shrdlu is the mischief-maker who lurks at the elbow of journalists and printers, causing a multitude of hilarious misprints, double meanings, and general mix-ups.

I also attribute to Gobfrey Shrdlu another type of curious happening, exemplified by the headlines 'ROSIE, 9, JOGGED BY SCHOOLFRIEND, SWALLOWS GOLDFISH', and 'WIFE AGREED TO BE HIT ON SATURDAYS'. In my first book for PAN, *Funny Ha Ha and Funny Peculiar*, these bizarre news items were the Funny Peculiars and were presented on the right-hand pages, while the Funny Ha Ha items (howlers and misprints) appeared on the left-hand pages.

I followed the same system in *Funny Ho Ho and Funny Fantastic* and in *Funny Amusing and Funny Amazing*, and here I am again with another collection of these two distinct types of shrdlidiocy – Funny Convulsing on the left-hand pages and Funny Confusing on the right.

In addition to the sources quoted in the text, I wish to acknowledge my debt to *Weekend*, *Punch*, and *The New Yorker*, in which some of the items first appeared. Special thanks to three enthusiastic shrdlologists: Edward North, Mary Pearce, and Patrick Moore, who have sent in many a gem from national and local newspapers. I have again borrowed a number of the best items from my *It Must Be True* series of Shrdlu books, published by Macdonald in the 1950s but long since out of print.

FUNNY CONVULSING

FUNNY CONFUSING

LADIES who have kindly undertaken to act as school crossing wardens are reminded again that if they attempt to carry out their duties without their clothing on motorists are unlikely to take notice of them.

Circular to school parents

Tom and I are like blood brothers. He means more to me than my own flesh and Mrs Denise Baines of Balaclava Road, Cambridge.

Cambridge News

The bride was held in place by a circlet of white flowers.

Surrey Advertiser

VISITORS

Husbands only. One per patient.

Sign in hospital

Last night a mini car swerved off the road and crashed into a lamp post in Magdalen Road, Bexhill. No casualties were reported, but communications on the 155-mile railway – only link between Addis Ababa and Djibouti – have been disrupted.

The Evening News

With reference to your telephone call regarding the live frogs sent you in error, we have cancelled our invoice for this dispatch, and sent five preserved specimens to you yesterday as arranged.

> Letter to a headmaster reprinted in
> *The Times Educational Supplement*

FARMERS in Taranaki, New Zealand, thought a mysterious new disease had struck when they suddenly found their cattle going blind. Then they discovered that the cows had been watching pipeline welders at work on the Kapuni natural gas pipelines.

Minister of Electricity Tom Shand commented: 'Nobody explained to the cows that it's dangerous to watch a welder at work unless you wear dark glasses'.

Now an Auckland firm has produced a 'Moonmaster' – a pair of welding glasses specially designed to fit cows, a must for every curious cow in New Zealand.

> *Safety and Rescue*

A young South Korean riding on the back of a giant sea turtle has been picked up by a Swedish cargo ship more than 100 miles off the Nicaraguan coast.

The Korean told the ship's captain that he had fallen into the Pacific from a Liberian ship. He climbed on to the turtle and clung to the shell for 15 hours.

The captain radioed to his company yesterday: 'We were quite shocked when we recognized a living human being riding on the back of a turtle. He fell unconscious to the deck, but a few minutes later he was able to speak.'

> *Daily Mail*

Men formed a chain and tried to light the fire with buckets of water.

Biggleswade Chronicle and Bedfordshire Gazette

Owners of 15 dogs released since July were ordered by the Agriculture Ministry to be muzzled. They must be exercised only on a lead and will stay under restriction six months.

Financial Times

STRIKEBOUND holidaymakers were kept waiting six hours for the jerry. Then it was filled to capacity.

Southern Echo

PASSENGERS HIT BY CANCELLED TRAINS

Manchester Evening News

BUGGED BED
WORSE THAN
BED BUG

says Attorney General

Headline in *Daily Mail*

A judge has ordered a man to stop writing alimony cheques to his divorced wife with the word 'adulteress' after her name. The judge, in New York, ruled: 'No woman should be put in the position of publishing a libel against herself in order to cash a cheque to which she is entitled.'

Daily Mirror

A MAN of 75 who went to hospital for an X-ray has found that he was shot in the hip 52 years ago – without knowing it. Doctors discovered the bullet when Mr John Philp, of Barnfield Road, Ealing, complained of arthritis. They decided not to remove it.

Mr Philp, a lance-corporal in the Black Watch during the First World War, was hit by rifle fire in Mesopotamia in 1917.

Daily Mail

Old soldier Bill Sawtell put hot poultices on the lump that he thought was a boil on his hip. Two days later the swelling went down – to reveal the tip of a bullet, 1½ ins long.

The bullet had taken twenty-four years to travel from his shoulder to his hip. And all the time 59-year-old Bill, of Abbotsbury-road, Weymouth, had no idea it was inside him.

As he waited for his wound to be dressed in hospital yesterday, he said: 'I was hit in the shoulder during an air raid over London as I was waiting to cross to Normandy in 1944'.

Daily Mirror

For her birthday he gave her a lunch of tulips and daffodils.

ABC Film Review

A Variety Concert was held on Wednesday at St Anthony's Theatre, Merchants' Quay, at 8 PM. The injured were taken to hospital, most of them with second and third degree burns.

Evening Press, Dublin

It is proposed to re-align the road to cut out a dangerous double bed which has been the scene of numerous serious accidents in recent years.

Oxford Times

The sleek, droop-nosed plane sped over the Arc de Elysees and across the Place de Triomphe, down the Champs la Concorde at about 1,500 ft before landing at Le Bourget.

Huddersfield Daily Examiner

WANTED

Some additional female technicians
at the fast-expanding Charles River
Breeding Laboratory. No previous
experience necessary.

Advert in Massachusetts paper

Glamour photographer with own equipment and good contacts seeks sleeping or active partner.

Advert in *The Stage*

Sacrificing accuracy somewhat recklessly for the sake of brevity, I am tempted to say that the object of the action is to determine which of these two bodies, if either, is the other, and, if not, whether either, and if so which, is another corporate body of the same name, or if not in fact such third body, is identical with it.

Law report

THE COMPUTER THAT HAD FLEAS

You wouldn't think computers could get fleas, would you? I mean they are such efficient machines you would expect them to come complete with de-lousing gear. But the computer owned by the Ministry of Agriculture and Fisheries in Guildford, Surrey, has had an attack of fleas.

It is a gleaming, modern affair, too, in a building as austere and sterile as a hospital ward. A hundred girls minister to the computer, and when they started to complain that they were getting fleabites, senior Ag and Fish men were sceptical. But a check showed the girls were right. There *were* fleas in the computer.

Some starlings had got trapped in the ventilating system, and when they died the fleas who lived off them turned their attention to the girls.

Sun

```
... In conclusion, Sir, I enclose
    my card and remains,
         Yours truly,
              VICTIM
```

The Market Mail

Seventy-one-year-old Mr Dearing, a bachelor, of Station Road, Staines, worked for 20 years as a production controller, and two years as sub-contracting manager. He was presented with his 41st clock by Mr Edward Snell, the boring shop superintendent.

Slough Observer

His gorgeous stage clothes and setting are pleasing to the eye, and his warm smile and disarming sense of humous add up to real professionalism.

Daily Mail

KENNETH HARLAN, FILM ACTOR, SAID TO HAVE BEEN SEEN WITH WIFE

Headline in *Portland Oregonian*

To relieve congestion, take Astoria ferry every fifteen minutes.

Advert on Queensboro Bridge, New York

This week 123 Glasgow Corporation drivers received medals for accident-free driving, 24 of them qualifying for the 15-year medal. Tommy already has tow bars on his 15-year medal.

Scottish Daily Express

Experts know that the alcoholic process takes longer in the men, but the end reshult ies the same.

Daily Record

One on the outside who criticizes the placement of square pegs in round holes should be sure that there are not more round holes and square pegs than there are square holes and round pegs. Even if this is not the case the critic should be certain that round holes are not a more serious problem than square ones, and he should withhold his criticism unless he is quite sure that it is better to leave round holes unfilled than it is to fill them partially with square pegs.

American Journal of Public Health

MAN SHOT DEAD BY HIS GUN DOG

Police last night named the killer of a man shot in the back. It was his gun dog, Sylvie. Police said Jean Marie Devaux, a 23-year-old hunter, placed his loaded rifle in the back seat of his car with Sylvie before going on an expedition near Le Havre, Northern France.

When he opened the door Sylvie sprang out, catching a paw in the trigger guard. The rifle went off, killing Devaux instantly. Tests on the rifle revealed Sylvie's paw print.

Daily Sketch

RAILWAY porter Bernard Hunt yesterday got his biggest tip in 12 years with British Rail – a 1962 grey Volkswagen van.

A passenger thrust the log book and test certificate into his hands as the 5.42 PM Blackpool–Manchester train pulled out of St Anne's station.

'It appears to be a legitimate gift,' police said. When the owner is traced, Mr Hunt, 55, of Glen Eldon Road, St Anne's, can have the van.

Daily Mail

The bride's bouquet was pink rose buds, and Heather Stephanotis. She was attacked by the Misses Louise Carlton, her niece, Fiona Danvers, Jennifer Burns and Angela Burns.

Crawley Advertiser

Pierced ears
3s 6d a pair

Sign in jeweller's shop

As the four finalists hit the last bend, he produced an electrifying bust which swept him past his opponents into the home straight to breast the tape.

Carmarthen Journal

Efforts to rescue three cows trapped halfway down 500-ft cliffs on the Dorset coast, near Lulworth, have been called off. A Defence Ministry statement said that they would be replaced by younger men.

West Lancashire Evening Gazette

MEDINA TO HAVE
PARENT TEACHER ASSASSINATION

Headline in *Medina (Oregon) Sentinel*

An astonishing book is to be published next month at a price of 15*s* – with most of its pages BLANK. *The Book of the Book* is the work of 45-year-old Idries Shah, author of several books on mysticism and magic who claims to be a direct descendant of the Prophet Mohammed.

Said Miss Sally Mallam, spokesman for the publishers, the Octagon Press, of Oxford Street, London: 'I think this book is so novel that there is every chance of it becoming a best-seller'. Including the contents, preface, fly and title pages the book contains only 1,326 words, spanning 14 pages. The other 260 sheets in the book, bound in red with gilt lettering, do not have a single printed letter on them.

The only clue to understanding the riddle of the empty sheets is in the sentence: 'When you realize the difference between the container and the content you will have knowledge'.

Sunday Mirror

There was still no trace today of two teenage Inverness-shire girls who have vanished from their homes. That means there will be no refuse collection on Monday.

Aberdeen Evening Express

MRS JOY EASTON wanted a 'lasting memorial' for her pet poodle's grave. A Cupid, perhaps, or a child holding a puppy, she thought. But sculptor Brian Hawker thought otherwise.

He made, delivered and erected over the grave in Mrs Easton's landscaped garden . . . a 7-ft high glass fibre lamp-post. Last night blonde Mrs Easton said at her home: 'I was both shocked and disgusted. I have told my gardener to take it down.'

Now she is refusing to pay Mr Hawker the 40 guineas still outstanding on his bill. Mr Hawker, 32, said: 'As I see it, the memorial needed to be something which a dog would appreciate. A lamp-post is among a dog's best friends.'

Daily Mail

ACCOMMODATION available. Will suit two working girls, willing to share room or young respectable working man.

Wisbech Standard

These thugs must be stopped and I intend to see that they are. Rule 4a in the council rent book says that parents must keep their parents under control.

The Daily Telegraph

As a small child she always had difficulty in tying cows in her ribbons and shoelaces.

New Zealand Weekly News

HOUSEHOLD AND MISCELLANEOUS FOR SALE...High Chair (converts to Electric Toaster) £3.10.0.

Royal Gazette, Bermuda

Princess Margaret, wearing a summery yellow-ribbed cotton dress, white brimmed hat covered with daisies and yellow sandals, was shown round the laboratories.

Oxford Times

I know boys will be boys, and I am not opposed to a modicum of high spirits after a successful match, but when it comes to scattering tintacks on the changing room floor, as your trainer I must really put my foot down.

From a Norfolk football club bulletin

When his wife refused to cook him a meal, a man cut the plugs off every electrical appliance in the house. She retaliated by attacking him with a stair-rod while he was in the lavatory.

Surrey Herald

Renewal notices for three books from Lincoln City library have come from the Saudi Arabian desert, where Mr Ronald Paing, a local schoolteacher, inadvertently took them on a nine months' stay in Mubbaraz. The books were treatises on central heating.

The Guardian

HERMANN SCHMIDT scribbled his will on a wall beside his bed just before he died. Yesterday, the 18-inch square section of wall was cut out and filed for probate in Philadelphia, America. Schmidt, a 49-year-old German immigrant, left his £4,250 estate to his belly-dancer fiancée, Genevieve Decker, 42.

His last scribbled words were: 'Genevieve, you take care of all my belongings. This gives you authority. Love, Hermann.' An earlier message gave the name and address of his doctor. But Schmidt, a glass polisher, was dead when police broke into his home.

Daily Mirror

A FOUR-LETTER word inspired a girl to strip naked yesterday. The girl, aged twenty-five, was fully clothed when she saw the word on a building sign . . . 'shed'.

So she did . . . and shed all her clothes. Then, without a stitch, she carried on walking along Euston Road, London. She was eventually driven off in a police car and later went to hospital. The girl told police that when she saw the sign she did 'what comes naturally'.

Daily Mirror

VANCOUVER: Dale Martin, an entertainer, has been ordered by a provincial court judge to avoid making anyone pregnant for the next three years. The order not to impregnate any girls came from Judge Leslie Bewley, who gave Martin a suspended sentence and the three-year probation for possession of an offensive weapon.

Toronto Globe

Mrs George was married before anaesthetics came into use in surgical operations.

Ludlow (Indiana) *Tribune*

Her husband said they hadn't really been fighting: 'We were arguing,' he claimed. Each defendant was fined £2. Wedding Bells Place an order for this journal with your newsagent and avoid disappointment.

Holborn and Finsbury Guardian

Student behaviour at Essex University, Colchester, 'makes *Lady Chatterly's Lover* like a vicarage tea party!' in comparison, Mr George Milsom, county councillor, said yesterday. Essex County Council agreed to cut their annual £107,000 grant by £1.

Daily Mail

'In the sixth form we've been trying to get uniform done away with. I think we'll soon be down to the boys just wearing a tie and the girls a grey skirt.'

Daily Mail

If you want to ride from your wedding in a horse-drawn coach, a Chinese rickshaw, a bicycle-made-for-two, Chitty-Chitty-Bang-Bang (the car of the film) or an elephant, apply to the Kensington Close Hotel. They will arrange it all.

Roger Williams, the young banqueting manager, was telling me yesterday that modern brides want something different for their weddings. He arranges transport, from elephants to tandems, through agents who do this kind of work. Costs a bit, of course. An elephant (ridden side-saddle) comes out at £100. A bicycle-made-for-two is only 10 guineas, but you have to provide your own bride-power.

A carriage and pair cost £25, but you can have a whole horse-drawn bus to take your guests with you for only £35. Chitty-Chitty-Bang-Bang is the most costly of the lot. Up to £200 for the day.

Henry Fielding in Sun

I was amazed to find that when I went to the toilet while on holiday in Salzburg I had to pay my money to a male attendant. But I was even more amazed when he started serenading me on his zither! How many women can boast they have been serenaded in the loo? – Miss G. Smith, Twickenham.

Letter in Sunday Mirror

THE HORNIMAN MUSEUM in South London, which has some 5,000 musical instruments, is kindly giving up one of its two pairs of genuine natural fibre poi balls. They are used to accompany traditional Hawaiian dances, and the Berenice Bishop museum in Honolulu is without a pair. Horniman is exchanging its balls for a nose flute, rattling gourd, rhythm sticks and a slit bamboo jingle.

The Guardian

The doctor smiled reassuringly at the worried mother and patted her little bot on the cheek.

Paperback book

They are selling whole chickens and portions already cooked, in wine, at 6*s* 3*d* a pound. All that is needed is to eat the chicken, while still sealed in the bag.

Liverpool Echo

```
Dear Sir,
   We are always glad to advise on humane
means of destruction for any species, but
in your case I think that this would
hardly be necessary.
```

Letter from animal welfare organization

☞ IN CASE OF FIRE, PLEASE DO YOUR UTMOST TO ALARM THE HALL PORTER

Notice in Austrian hotel

Dear Sirs,
   I am getting married soon and would like to know what causes this to happen and if there is a way of preventing it.

Letter received by Kodak Ltd

Soon after the war broke out I sailed from Tilbury on a merchant ship bound for Australia. I had written to my mother, but hadn't been able to post it so, as the ship was passing Southend, my hometown, I dropped the addressed letter overboard in a beer bottle.

Arriving in Australia, I received a letter from my mother, saying that a woman had found my bottle at Sheerness and had forwarded the letter.

On a later voyage and passing the same spot I 'posted' another bottled letter to my mother. Unfortunately we were sunk and I finished up in a German POW camp. So it was some time before I learned that my second letter had been found and forwarded – by the same woman!

My mother still has those two letters in her 'treasure chest'. – A. GRAY, Great Cambridge Road, Enfield, Middlesex.

Letter in Daily Mirror

HUSBAND MIAOWS UNDER THE BED

The cat noises that came from under a young wife's bed kept her awake for months. They also gave her a headache – for the plaintive mewing was being made not by a cat, but by her husband. Every night, instead of getting into bed, he curled up under it . . . and just miaowed.

In desperation the wife asked a lawyer if she had grounds for a separation. 'My husband is a good and kind man, but rather shy,' she said. 'When it gets dark he stops talking and starts miaowing.' The astonished lawyer decided that the only complaint she could give was: 'My husband thinks he is a cat and prefers to sleep under, not in, my bed.'

Now a court in Imperia, Italy, will be asked to decide whether a husband's miaows in the night constitute grounds for legal separation.

Daily Mirror

Mr and Mrs Fred Upton returned Thursday from a visit in the tropics. The rest and change of climate has done them both good. Mrs Upton looks healthier and lonelier than ever.

New England weekly

Miss Edith Seymour Clark, daughter of Mrs Howard Gates Clark of 983 Park Lane, will be carried on the afternoon of April 21st to Mr John Jacob Gunther, of 46 East 81 Street, in Christ Church.

The World

CUSTOMERS GIVING ORDERS WILL BE PROMPTLY EXECUTED

Notice in Bombay tailor's

It was while walking home, one raw morning, from an all-night party that she caught a child.

Irish Independent

The dangers of the Taupo-Napier road were also brought home to us as it was on the metalled part of this road that we saw the only two accidents during our tour. One was the overturned petrol tanker blazing away with the hillsides in flames around it. The other was a saloon car carrying women and children upside down at the side of the road.

Napier (NZ) *Daily Telegraph*

HOME FOR OLD CARS
– AND LOBSTERS

From NESTA ROBERTS, Paris, August 13th

Each year French oyster and mussel beds produce a harvest approaching 120,000 tons – the figure for 1965 was 116,000. For lobsters and crabs which cannot be cultivated in the same way, the 1965 figure was a mere 16,000 tons, and even so there was a danger of over-exploiting the limited stocks. Now, off the coast of Palavas, in the Languedoc, there has been launched an experiment which may help to redress the situation.

It is the brainchild of M. Doumenge, Professor of Geography at the University of Montlellier. Crustacea, he knew, were attracted to old iron, in the sense that they established themselves in wrecks. If steel hulls, why not a metal chassis? In other words, if old cars due for the scrapyard could find an ocean graveyard, would that not, besides solving the problem of their disposal, provide nesting places for lobsters which would encourage them to breed?

M. Doumenge succeeded in interesting the university's productivity centre in his plan. Its principal obtained the rights over 10 hectares of the Mediterranean off Palavas-les-Flots, where derelict cars will be sunk at a depth of 15 to 18 metres.

There, it is hoped, nestling in the boot of a Bentley, sandwiched among the gears of a DS, lobster and langoustine will flourish and multiply. As a sideline it is thought that this marine cemetery, such as Valéry never dreamed of, may also prove an attraction to skin-divers.

The Guardian

Police Sgt Stanley Minshall found a woman lying screaming inside a telephone kiosk. Her husband was there, and the sergeant asked him why she was in this state. The husband attacked him and the woman joined in the attack. 'This is a classic example of what sometimes happens when a police officer tries to stop a husband striking his wife,' commented Insp R. Jones.

Birkenhead News

AT STUD George S—, LRAM Teacher of Pianoforte, Theory, Harmony, Accompaniment.

Keighley News

FURNISHED FRONT airy room near bust stop suitable for bachelors. Apply 4 Benji Road, Kuala Lumpur.

Straits Times

HAIRCUTTING
WHILE YOU
WAIT

Notice in Dublin barber's

WOODEN BENCHES for the crucial fourth India–Australia Test in Calcutta have been replaced by cricket officials.

Daily Express

When police found him with the two girls he said that one was a piece and the other a neighbour.

The Evening News

9.5 SHERLOCK HOLMES as Dr Watson in 'STUDY IN SCARLET'.

Advert in Dublin *Evening Herald*

Bus conductor KK 46793 had never stopped his No 19 double-decker so that a passenger could enjoy the view – until yesterday. And he had never been asked if he was an impostor – until yesterday.

But then he had never had a passenger riding-to-rule in protest against the busmen's work-to-rule. The protest began with a loud roar, as the green Hants & Dorset bus left Westover Road, Bournemouth. It was ex-Civil Servant Mr Kampara Ahmed announcing to the conductor that he intended to pay his fare – in accordance with Section 5 of the rule book.

Mr Ahmed, 75, bearded and clutching a walking stick, produced a £1 for his 2s 11d fare. First he wanted to know: 'Are you the conductor?' Uniformed conductor KK 46793 replied: 'No, I'm a lorry-driver'. 'Well then,' said Mr Ahmed, 'where is your authorization from the traffic commissioners?'

Eventually the ticket was given. Then came another pause. Under Section 6, the conductor must duly assure the passenger that the ticket is new. Then, under the statutory orders and regulations covering public service vehicles, Mr Ahmed asked for the bus to be stopped at a request stop. He did not want to get off. The rule book doesn't say he has to.

When the time came for Mr Ahmed to leave the bus, Section 4 of the rule book made his duty clear. He had to stay in his seat until the bus was stationary. This accomplished it was time for peace talks, the offer to shake hands. But it was refused. Said conductor KK 46793: 'I don't have to shake hands with you or give you my name. *It's not in the regulations.*'

Daily Mail

MARSEILLES. Seaman Marcel Rivien has won a breach-of-promise suit brought against him by red-head Noelle Michel. He told the court he could not marry a girl with 12 tattoos on her chest.

Weekend

(We all have faults of character and I cannot conceal from readers that Gobfrey Shrdlu has pronounced sadistic tendencies. This is evident from many items I have chronicled in *Funny Ha Ha and Funny Peculiar* and its two successors: 'When the baby has finished its bottle, drop it in a saucepan of water and boil it'. 'MAN STOWS AWAY TO SEE GIRL FRIED' 'She wrinkled up her face as her daughter pinned a rose on it for the photograph.' 'Securely pierced by a brass toasting fork she held a piece of bread to the fire.' 'VOLUNTEER WORKERS PUT IN CHURCH HEATING PLANT' and so on.

Five more items of this kind have accumulated, I am sorry to say, and I give these below. – D.P.)

Eleven tents were pitched and nearly 20 youngsters converged on the camping site. Wood was chopped and a general purpose fire lit under Mr Tom Watson, and the drizzly atmosphere was soon flavoured with the scent of wholesome sizzling.

Crawley and District Observer

Mr John McCutcheon is married to Susan Dart of New Orleans instead of going to Australia as he requested.

New Orleans paper

The bride was very upset when one of her little attendants accidentally stepped on her brain and tore it.

Kent Messenger

Request largest possible attendance
my trial, Monday, October 6th, Tax
Court 26, Federal Square, for non-
payment of income taxes. I will re-
present myself. No lawyer retained
by me. I can be recognized by four
missing front teeth and dislocated
left shoulder.

Advert in The New York Times

'PREGNANT' FOR 37 YEARS
By Our Rome Correspondent

A peasant woman aged 72, carried an unborn eight months old baby in her body for 37 years without being aware of it. Prof Vito de Palma, chief obstetrician of the Termoli Hospital, Campobasso, in South Italy, disclosed yesterday.

He said that the woman, named only as Maria T. came to his surgery a few days ago complaining of stomach pains. X-rays revealed the presence of an eight months old child whose body was completely fossilized.

The Daily Telegraph

LAST MONDAY a garage fitted a new radio aerial to my car. I have now discovered that I have five different ways of turning off my radio. They are: (1) by operating the foot brake; (2) by changing gear; (3) by touching the loudspeaker cover; (4) by tapping the speedometer glass; and (5) the on-off switch.

I also find that I can increase the volume by operating the heater control. I doubt if any of the expensive cars at this year's Motor Show have such an elaborate radio system incorporated!

Letter in Sunday Mirror

Mr F— sustained severe bruising, his wife had three stitches inserted in a forehead laceration. Julie had a fractured collarbone and Gary facial bruises, which caused rejoicing.

Pocklington Times

I felt my hair being yanked cruelly as I tumbled to the ground. Audrey's hate-crazed face hoovered over me.

Modern Confessions

In a recent report of a competition held at one of Pontin's holiday camps it was inadvertently stated that it was for 'elephant' grandmothers instead of elegant grandmothers. We apologize to Mrs Helen P—, who gained the third place, for any embarrassment this may have caused.

Stockport Advertiser

EVANS SAYS PUTTING MAN
TO DEATH ELIMINATES
HOPE OF REHABILITATION

Olympia (Wash.) *Olympian*

For the past many years I've huffed and puffed when struggling with rubbers and overshoes, both for my plum self and wriggling spaghetti-legged youngster.

No more!

I now put the shoes inside of chicken over certain vegetables. Mushroom soup is the rain boots first then step is good with peas in the shoes. Sure is easier.

Nyack (NY) *Journal-News*

RABBIT IN MIXER SURVIVES

A baby rabbit fell into a quarry's mixing machine yesterday and came out in the middle of a concrete block. But the rabbit still had the strength to dig its way free before the block set.

The tiny creature was scooped up with 30 tons of sand, then swirled and pounded through the complete mixing process. Mr Michael Hooper, the machine operator, found the rabbit shivering on top of the solid concrete block, its coat stiff with fragments. A hole from the middle of the block and paw marks showed the escape route.

Mr Reginald Denslow, manager of J. R. Pratt and Sons' quarry at Kilmington, near Axminster, Devon, said: 'This rabbit must have a lot more than nine lives to go through this machine. I just don't know how it avoided being suffocated, ground, squashed or cut in half.' With the 30 tons of sand, it was dropped into a weighing hopper and carried by conveyor to an overhead mixer where it was whirled around with gallons of water.

From there the rabbit was swept to a machine which hammers wet concrete into blocks by pressure of 100 lb per square inch. The rabbit was encased in a block 18 inches long, nine inches high and six inches thick. Finally the blocks were ejected on to the floor to dry and the dazed rabbit clawed itself free. 'We cleaned him up, dried him by the electric fire, then he hopped away,' Mr Denslow said.

The Daily Telegraph

LUCIO SILVEIRA, 30, fell asleep on a heap of pitch left by road workers in Sao Paulo and woke up as a statue. The warmth of his body softened the pitch and he sank deeper and deeper until only his head and shoulders were showing. When he awoke the pitch had solidified and he looked like a bust mounted on a black base.

The fire brigade cut a block out of the pitch and carted Lucio to hospital, where nurses took more than an hour to remove the pitch.

The Guardian

Councillor Mrs Hallinan said the education authority had set up various nits in different parts of Cardiff.

South Wales Echo

The Rev Robert Rebhahn, Dean of Students, said a dormitory now housing freshmen women would be closed and two floors of a 1-storey men's dormitory would be opened to women students next fall.

Father Rebhahn said the step was being taken for economy and would save the school $50,000 a year.

St Louis Post Dispatch

FERRARI . . . extensive mechanical overhaul, discs, humorous expensive extras.

Exchange & Mart

David Ernest M— was paid £5 for having no licence for his van and £8 for speeding.

Lancashire Evening Telegraph

FOR SALE. BEAUTIFUL litter pedigree wire Fox Terrier
        Puppies.
        BLACK Pedigree Pram: good condition. Write
        Box 888.

Burton Daily Mail

AIRLINE STOPS FOR A MOUSE

The pilot of a Britannia airliner brought his plane to a halt while taxiing for take-off yesterday to avoid hitting a mouse. The 112-seat plane, owned by the BKS airline, was setting out on a flight from Newcastle upon Tyne to London. Passengers were not told why the pilot stopped the airliner. A spokesman for BKS said later: 'He saw a mouse run across in front of the plane and pulled up to let it pass'.

He added: 'I have been in aviation for 22 years, but I have never heard of an action like this before'. The take-off was delayed only a few seconds and the incident was described in the plane's log as 'delayed due to conflicting traffic'.

Sun

Our picture shows Miss Leena Brusiin, 22, from Helsinki, who has won the Miss Europe 1968 contest in Kinshasa, Congo. The contest, with 21 competitors, was held in Kinshasa because arrangements for it to be staged in Nice were interrupted by riots in France in May.

The Daily Telegraph

POSITION WANTED. Dour-faced, lazy, unpersuasive male offers only honesty, loyalty and some intelligence for £2,000 a year. Write Box No ...

The Times

Fruit vendor Tiago Machado, who was reported to have seen 'little green men' come out of a flying saucer when it landed near Sao Paulo, said yesterday that he had been misquoted. They were little red men, he declared.

Sussex paper

Preston went to Craven Cottage encouraged by three successive away wins. They finished up adding another triumph at the expense of a team considered invisible at home.

Sunday Post

John F—, the celebrated singer, was in a motor-car accident last week. We are happy to state he was able to appear the following evening in four pieces.

Bradford paper

AT Southborne, well-built detached house in sheltered position yet with sea views, adjoining bus route and short walk to shops. Immediate possession. 3 good bedrooms, two spacious deception rooms.

Bournemouth Evening Echo

MAN KILLED BY HIPPO

A Monze villager has been killed by a hippo on the Kafue river. Mr Mutti Kandemba of Mukana Village died after the hippo charged at him while rowing a boat.

Times of Zambia

A 17-year-old boy died in the New Plymouth hospital as a result of injuries received in a car crash at Inglewood. He was Rex Manton, who died less than two hours after the accident. His condition was reported tonight to be satisfactory.

Hamilton Times, New Zealand

MAN TRAPPED BY BEDSPRINGS
FOR 5 DAYS

Mr Leonard Alcock, 63, of Britannia Road, Sheffield, was held prisoner for five days without food and water when his 30-year-old bed collapsed, plunging him among the mass of tangled springs. Neighbours who realized he had not left home since last Wednesday, called the police.

Mr Alcock was released by ambulance men and taken to the Royal Hospital, Sheffield, given a check up and a good meal and allowed to return home. He said yesterday: 'I went to bed to listen to the Celtic match on the radio last Wednesday and fell asleep. When I woke up I was down among the springs.

'I kept struggling to get free but the springs were too strong for me. I don't know what I would have done if the police hadn't come because I was getting weaker.'

The Daily Telegraph

If he's stopped breathing, remove any obstruction such as false teeth or food, and immediately apply the 'kiss-of-life' (mouth-to-mouth breathing), the technique of which I'll describe next month.

Family Circle

When parties of visitors used to go round newspaper offices, someone on the staff would always give them a thrill by shouting: 'Hold the front page'. Nobody took any notice but the visitors liked it. 'Just like the films,' they said, and went home happy.

The shrimp peelers at Thunderbolt in Georgia have been joining in a similar game. Now they are tired of it, but their bosses are not. So the men went to court and got the judge to order their employers not to make them sing 'The Shrimp Boats Are A'Coming' every time visitors tour the factory.

Reveille

Mr Hammond said he would guess the cost of installing the new shunt in each substation between New York and Washington would be between $35,000 and $50,000 and that the world could start in two weeks and be completed in 16 to 20 weeks.

The New York Times

WEST BROMWICH ... Freehold House ... fitted kitchen (sink unit, plumber in Bendix washing machine) ...

West Bromwich Midland Chronicle and Free Press

> **'You can fool some of the people all the time, and all the people some of the time, but you can't fool all the people all the time.' That is the idea on which our business has been built up.**

Advert in *Johannesburg Daily Mail*

Councillor A. J. Rabson told Monday's meeting of the rural council: 'Today was the first day for nine days that some residents have been able to use their toilets. Something has got to be done very soon to relieve this situation.'

Folkestone Herald

Bang! It's the amazing
exploding lady

It was Christmas time in the hospital. And hardly a sound was heard. Until two doctors, visiting patients on their hospital round, heard a crack 'like a pistol shot' ring out.

'We found no commotion and no prematurely pulled Christmas cracker,' Doctors C. Evans and B. J. Ridyard say today in a letter to the *British Medical Journal*. Instead there was a timid woman of 40 – Mrs A— who called out apologetically that it was her and her capsules.

The doctors had discovered the Amazing Case of the Inoffensive Exploding Lady, who goes off with a bang once daily. Mrs A— explained that she is taking duagastrone, a special preparation which her family doctor told her would heal her duodenal ulcer. But three to seven hours after taking a capsule, there would be a loud 'shot' in her bowels, say the doctors, who write from Liverpool's Royal Southern Hospital.

It wasn't very convenient either, since Mrs A— exploded at the most unlikely times. She and her husband spent many sleepless nights, waiting for an explosion around 2 am, following their evening meal at 7 pm. And the awful climax came when a television repair man called at Mrs A—'s house. As he was tuning the set the lady went off with a bang.

The stunned repair man dropped his tools, pulled the wires from the socket and searched in vain for a short circuit. Baffled, he 'turned suspiciously towards Mrs A—' then suggested that the metal springs of her settee had broken. He stripped down the sofa to investigate the upholstery. And Mrs A—, too shy to tell him of her complaint, stood by and watched.

The doctors tell Mrs A—'s story today in an attempt to discover if she is unique. And to warn others. Just in case the trouble should blow up again.

Sun

Tobacco stocks are down. Chewing gum stocks are up. And the brains of the world are trying to leapfrog to some conclusions as to what could possibly replace cigarette smoking as a nervous to what could possibly replace cigarette smoking as a nervous habit.

World-Telegram Sun

WANTED, Solicitor, experienced in laundry or dye works, to drive wagon.

Vancouver World

Confused by the noise of traffic, a cow that probably was experiencing its first taste of city life, got mixed up with vehicles in Milwaukee Avenue yesterday and was struck by a street car. It was so badly injured that Patrolman Stegmiller ended his life with a bullet.

Detroit News

Mr E. G. Winterton, headmaster, would not comment on the threat. However, he did say: 'Some children have been behaving very childishly'.

Doncaster Post

The Rev W. L. Johnson will start for his annual holiday on June 13th. He therefore asks that the Missionary Boxes be returned to him not later than June 10th.

Parish magazine

Firemen took nearly an hour to release pallbearer Mr John Earlfield who got a leg jammed between the coffin and the graveside at Kings Cross Methodist Church, Halifax.

Coventry Evening Telegraph

Stockholm police are looking for a thief who took a small house from a Stockholm suburb.

Herald Tribune

Russian medical student Sergei Kelnikov has claimed a world record – after kissing a pig non-stop for 23 min 14 sec.

Tit-Bits

Judge H. D. Lang of Perth County has ruled that an election in nearby Mornington Township was valid even though a deputy returning officer milked his cows before returning a ballot box.

London Ontario Free Press

I must be one of the very few people who have bitten a gorilla. It happened when I was a keeper of the ape house at London Zoo. Laden with bottles of milk – a usual nightcap for the apes – I was passing the gorilla cage when an arm stretched through the bars and gripped my shoulder with paralysing strength. The gorilla seemed to be saying: 'Give me the lot, or else!'

My reflex action was to bite him. Immediately he sprang back, ruefully rubbing the arm on which my puny teeth could have made no impression. After serving the other animals, I made sure that the gorilla had an extra helping of milk to salve his lost dignity.

It took a long time for me to live down a reputation as 'the man who bit the gorilla'. By the way, gorillas do not taste very nice. – S. R. Troy, Winchmore Hill.

Letter in Reveille

Just to keep the record straight, it was the famous Whistler's Mother, not Hitler's, that was exhibited at the recent meeting of Pleasantville Methodists. There is nothing to be gained in trying to explain how the error occurred.

Titusville (Pa.) Herald

Donald's father told the court that his son's personality had completely changed since the accident. His career in the catering industry was finished because of the accident and he still carried a chip on his shoulder.

Kentish Gazette

FOUND, White Fox-terrier Dog. Apply with name on collar, to 51 Park Rd, Regents Park.

The Daily Telegraph

CHEAP SPONGE ROLL

Take a teacupful of flour and mix it with a teacupful of caster sugar and a teaspoonful of baking powder; break two eggs into a cup, then slide into the mixture.

Bristol Times and Mirror

Can you advise me what can be done to rid my house of earwigs? Last year we were alive with them. We used to find them on our bed, and used to run down the wall and across the table at mealtimes.

Letter in *Amateur Gardening*

WASHINGTON: Two masked gunmen made a surburban congregation sing hymns – including *Trust and Obey* – while their purses and wallets were being emptied.

Daily Mail

In a recent *Opportunity Knocks* programme Hughie Green asked a sponsor of one of the entertainers how long a correspondence game of chess might take. A friend in Germany and I are in the middle of a game that began in 1914! We have only just made our 32nd move, but a stupid mistake I made in my last move threatens to bring the game to an untimely end. – W. F. Gross, Finsbury Park.

Letter in TV Times

A man who attacked a tailor's dummy in the window of a high street store acted from public spirit, not dishonesty, magistrates at Ryde, Isle of Wight, decided yesterday.

Mr Tom Lane, 36, a Scot, who pleaded not guilty to shopbreaking, said he was on his way home at midnight after Hogmanay. 'I heard a crash of glass from the shop. I saw two men running away and spotted what I thought was another man in the window. I crawled through the hole in the glass and leapt on him.'

When they crashed to the floor he realized the man was a dummy. He was so convulsed with laughter that he was still lying there when the police arrived. Lane was found not guilty and discharged.

The Daily Telegraph

JAMES CAMPBELL of Kinley Park House, Perth, is not sending Christmas Cards this year as nobody sent him any last year.

Personal column, The Times

Over the range from about 450 degrees centigrade to upwards of 500 degrees centigrade, the coal passes through a phase of elasticity during which it can be moulded between the fingers like putty.

The Elements of Fuel Technology

A Jersey heifer aged 26 months and owned by Mr E. Loxmore, was left in a very weak condition last weekend after giving birth to quadrupeds.

Korumburra Times

Any member striking a shuttlecock with his or her racquet while lying on the floor, shall be subject to a fine of 3*d*.

Rules of Winchester Badminton Club

Anita Ekberg and Rick Van Nutter just ran up (a record) five years of marriage. They celebrated on their boat – an exact replica of a Chinese junk, which they had built in Hong Kong, off the coast of Cannes.

Scranton (Pa.) *Tribune*

All you do is tip everything off the plates down the drain and the machine grinds it all into easily digestible particles.

South Wales Echo

They will both be put out in the panda pit again today and zoo officials will take a closer look at each other.

Derby Evening Telegraph

A HAPPY husband set off on holiday on his motor-cycle combination yesterday – and left his wife standing. Ten miles from his home in Manchester he realized his mistake and got the RAC to pass on a message saying he was returning to collect her.

Sunday Mirror

CONFERENCE 1969
In view of the Executive Council's decision to hold the 1969 Conference at Plymouth the Institute has made the necessary arrangements to hold the Conference at Hastings.

Journal of the Institute of Shops Acts Administration

Pathologist Dr Malcolm Cameron said Miss T— died from multiple injuries including a fractured spine.

Mr Mayne said: 'I have never envisaged the King's Arms as a tourist hotel. It is the sort of place one might stay for a few nights but she had been there several weeks. There are certain signs of eccentricities. It is not usual for a woman of 24 to leave her clothes in the bathroom and walk 35 to 40 ft to her bedroom unclothed.'

Evening Standard

'I have a pet budgerigar which has a swing in its cage. I have made a practice of disconnecting its swing each Sunday and not putting it back into use until Monday morning. Is this in accord with strict Christian principle?'

Quoted in *New Statesman*'s 'This England' column

To emphasize the shape of the eyes, pencil in a fine brown line actually following the growth of the lashes. Mascara must be made into a nice creamy consistency and lower lashes made up well with lemon curd and ice the top with lemon water icing, or sprinkle icing sugar on top.

Greenock Telegraph

Word was received last week that Mrs Gertrude Higgins, teacher of the 36th Street School, was severely bitten by a dog on the school grounds. Principal Gail Mahoney observed that it could just as easily have been a child.

Los Angeles South-West News-Press

Police are anxious to interview a well-built man, 5 ft 10 ins to 6 ft tall, wearing dark-coloured clothing and no raincoat.

The Star (Sheffield)

Hampshire elected to bath first on a pitch damp on top from the early morning rain.

Wolverhampton Express and Star

If you shoot yourself and have not used Blank's Ammunition, you have missed one of the pleasures of life.

Advert in Birmingham paper

LANDLORD Fred Williams noticed something odd about his yellow Labrador, Misty. The dog looked as pleased as Punch as it walked around . . . grinning. But Mr Williams couldn't even raise a smile – for Misty was wearing her master's false teeth.

Mr Williams, of High Road, Ipswich, had left his teeth on the table. Misty, feeling peckish before breakfast, grabbed them. But she had bitten off more than she could chew – even with those extra molars. Mr Williams got them back – after a struggle. He managed to get them repaired and at opening time his normal smile was resumed.

Daily Mirror

> *In order to maintain a high standard of service to our customers, this branch will be closed all day on Thursdays.*

Sign in shop in Walton-on-Thames

● For two months the sewer in the main street of Lakehurst, New Jersey, was clogged up. Workmen discovered that an outsize bra was causing the trouble.

Tit-Bits

EX-SAILOR Pierre Cadiou, a restaurant owner at Guidel, Brittany, sends orders for lobsters to his wholesaler by semaphore. He made this arrangement with the supplier – also an ex-naval man – because, he says, the French telephone system is so bad.

The People

He looked almost square, as if his tailor had put too much pudding in the shoulders.

Toronto Star

Observing the temporary incapacity of Mr Lea who seemed to be thinking furiously with his mouth open, Mr Swift MacNeill filled the aching void.

Liverpool Courier

After all, we are largely as nature made us, and Governor Smith's smile was born with him, just as were his liking for children and his derby hat.

Omaha Evening World-Herald

Formerly a don at Oxford, he developed later an interest in education, and migrated to Ontario.

Canadian Review

Wreckage is being washed ashore at Abermawr, Pembroke-shire. It is feared there has been a wreck.

Morning Leader

Blackpool, bed/breakfast, 17s 6d – Mrs Davenport £6.

Middlesex Advertiser and Gazette

Cooler in the South, Warmer in the South is the seven-day forecast of the *Sunday Express* weather experts.

Sunday Express

In the desert, as one might expect, a lot of discomfort is caused by the lack of water, intensified by the extreme heat. We have found our own conservation solution though – we use vodka to clean our teeth and degassed lemonade for washing. We have tried reversing this combination but find that the skin absorbs the vodka, putting us in a drunken stupor, and the lemonade froths when mixed with toothpaste, making it difficult to rinse away. Do not worry too much about expense – the lemonade costs more than the vodka!

From a field engineer's report
quoted in Redifon Star

PATNA Dec. 1st.

A frail but handsome middle-aged woman, who waited for a long 20 years in a corner of the third class waiting hall of the Patna Junction Railway Station where she took up abode waiting for her lover whom she had missed during a train journey, died quietly in her sleep on Monday.

Nothing could be ascertained about her antecedents though her continued stay over the years had become the talk of the town. Two scrappy notes written in Hindi found in her old and damaged steel trunk gave the clue to her tragedy.

She quietly lay on her rickety charpoi and waited and waited seldom opening her lips and grew thinner and thinner till death claimed her. A one-eyed sadhu, who kept her company for some years, disappeared quietly after her body was consigned to the holy Gnaga by the railway police.

The refrain of her jottings on two crumpled pieces of paper yellow with age, was 'Kab awoge ji? Kahan ho? Intazaar karti, bahoot din ho gaye'. (When will you come? Where are you? . . . I have waited for you long.) Whoever she was, it was apparent from her dress and demeanour that she came from a well-to-do respectable family. About Rs. 500 in currency notes and some ornaments were found in her street trunk after her death.

Indian paper

COOK WANTED, March 1st. Comfortable room with radio; two in family; only one who can be well recommended.

Advert in Hereford Paper

The winner of the competition to guess the number of sweets in the jar was Mrs— who will therefore travel to Majorca by air, spend five days in a luxury hotel (all inclusive) and fly home via Paris, without any need to spend a penny.

Announcement in a Westmorland church magazine

Lady with one child 2½ years old seeks situation as house-keeper. oGod cook.

Advert in S. African Paper

... the bride wore a Spanish influenced dress with high neck, and frills on the sleeves ... The dress which was gathered at the back fell gently to the floor.

Middlesex Advertiser and Gazette

Rev J. Towney Davis has spoken in the largest Baptist churches in America. To miss hearing him will be the chance of a lifetime.

Raleigh (N Carolina) *News & Observer*

Walter Hornbaker, South Fayette St, bagged a 4-point buck, Robert Thomas, RRI, bagged a 6-point buck, and Billy Dovey of Loudon Rd.

Mercersburg (Pennsylvania) *Journal*

After eight years' searching the Parish Register for a name to match the initials H. W. P. on a stone slab in his church, the Rev Phillip Randall, of Eye, near Peterborough, has solved the mystery. The initials stand for Hot Water Pipe.

Sunday Mirror

Milkman

When you leave the milk will you please put coal on the fire, let the dog out, and put newspaper inside the door.

P.S. Don't leave any milk

Recently my husband and I went to view an old cottage that was for sale. Upstairs I turned to see my husband staring at two photographs on the wall. To my amazement he told me they were photographs of his father and mother, before they married. We later discovered that the house had belonged to one of his mother's cousins whom he had never met. – Mrs E. Moore, Bradford, Yorks.

Letter in *Weekend*

PIPELINE RAPTURED

Algeria state-owned pipeline from the Sahara oil-fields to the Mediterranean port of Arzew near Oran has been raptured, Reuter quoted reliable sources as saying in Algiers.

Ghanaian Times

The bridesmaids were the bride's sister, Miss Elizabeth C—, who is also an actress and is about to start a child.

Surrey Herald

A proposal of the Harrisburg Redevelopment Authority involving possible demolition of the city's new planner when he takes office next Friday, it was indicated yesterday.

Harrisburg (Pennsylvania) *Patriot*

The speaker told of his adventure with a perilous bra constrictor.

Methodist Newsletter

In the absence of the Vicar of Newton Poppleford, the Rev 7ZN811851 7ZT451870 7ZZ770891 R. G. M—, who will be on holiday.

Exeter Express and Echo

She caught a bug at the top of the road and it carried her to the Elephant and Castle.

South London Press

Nineteen-year-old Texan Roger Martinez set a world record by swallowing 225 live goldfish in 42 minutes in a San Antonio contest. His prize: a free fish dinner.

Sun

That James Bartley, an AB of the *Star of the East* was in 1891 swallowed by a whale and was recovered alive from it several hours after.

It is far beyond my comprehension how this story, and a similar Biblical one, can be credited (for even a moment) by anyone having a most limited knowledge of physics and physiology, though it is said that some old lady said that she had no difficulty in believing that Jonah was swallowed by a whale, and that if it had been reported that Jonah swallowed the whale, she would have believed that too!

The Bartley story was unfortunately reported in *Sixty-three Years of Engineering* (1924), by Sir Francis Fox, MICE. I reviewed that interesting book for the Journal of the Society of Engineers, October–December 1925, and could not let the story pass unchallenged. From internal evidence it was shown how impossible the story was. Four years later it was pleasing to learn that the story of Jonah and the whale was repudiated in *A New Commentary on Holy Scripture* of which the Editor in chief was Bishop Gore. In 1925 I put a query in *Notes and Queries* and on 16th January 1926 Canon A. Lukyn Williams replied stating that he had investigated the matter in 1906 and decided that the Bartley story was 'a *canard* pure and simple'. In *The Daily Telegraph* of February 27th, 1928, Albert R. Steggall of Holy Trinity Vicarage, S Shields, wrote stating that the wife of the captain of the *Star of the East* had refuted the story. Still more facts are available, but we must end and do so with another story, viz, that when Jonah felt himself in the power of the whale, he was down in the mouth and felt he was going to blubber!

from *Popular Fallacies* by A. S. E. Ackerman

She could not say on which side of the road he was riding in Commissioner Street, but he turned into West Street on the wrong side. She was sure that after the accident she fell onto the pavement on the correct side of the road.

Johannesburg Star

Mr & Mrs Simon P—
request the honour of your
presents at the marriage
of their daughter Eve to
Mr James J—

Wedding invitation

They took with them an Irish terrier dog and a brown sheep dog – both pets. Both were wearing horn-rimmed glasses.

Manchester paper

Jenkins, it is claimed, was driving at a high rate of speed and swerving from side to side. As he approached the crossing he started directly towards it and crashed into Miss Miller's rear end which was sticking out into the road about a foot. Luckily she escaped injury and the damage can easily be remedied with a new coat of paint.

Ohio paper

A woman's leg was auctioned for 3s yesterday – a penny an inch. The 3-ft artificial leg was among lost property handed in to the police at North Walsham, Norfolk.

Sun

CANADIAN typist Chamber Landis, 23, has often had her leg pulled about her unusual Christian name. But it will be worse now. She has just married Vancouver salesman Les Potts.

Tit-Bits

The advantages that mother's milk holds over other forms of milk have never been better stated than in the schoolgirl's alleged answer to a domestic science question:

1. It's cleaner.
2. It's cheaper.
3. The cat can't get at it.

Letter in *The Observer*

CALGARY, Alberta, June 3rd. – Mr William Holmberg was working on his lawn when geese started falling all around him. He said he heard the honking overhead of a flight of Canada geese, and 'the next minute they started to drop'.

Eight of the birds fell over an area of about half a block. One of them crashed through the roof of a house, causing damage estimated at about £80. Others fell into gardens and in the street.

Mr Holmberg said: 'The birds were in perfect shape. There does not seem to be any reasonable explanation why they dropped. I thought they had eaten poisoned grain.' Officials from the fish and game branch were equally puzzled. They have sent six of the birds to Edmonton for examination. – Reuter.

Mrs Lukes was caught beneath the auto and taken to St Joseph's Hospital with several fractured bones. The bones were on their way to Woonsocket to spend their holiday.

Connecticut paper

When the baby is done drinking it must be unscrewed and laid in a cool place under a tap. If the baby does not thrive on fresh milk it should be boiled.

Women's magazine

Soon after the Rev B. P. Mohan, Vicar of St John's arrived in Penge in 1936, a series of national events took place which started with the destruction by fire of the Crystal Palace and culminated with the outbreak of war in 1939.

Beckenham & Penge Advertiser

RESTAURANT SUR LA MER
Aujourd'hui . . . L'Iris-Stew a l'Ecossaise

Notice outside French restaurant

SIR WILLIAM RAMSAY'S POSER STARTLES
AUDIENCE

London, February 4th. Sir William Ramsay raised the question whether the unfit should be left to die at the annual dinner of the Institute of Sanitary Engineers tonight.

Montreal Gazette

A REVERSING lorry hit a gaslamp standard in Bradford yesterday and gas began hissing from a broken joint. Firemen used an emergency plug to stem it – a cucumber from a nearby greengrocer's.

Daily Express

A Dorset firm who make chastity belts have been told that the belts are classed as furniture and must carry purchase tax of $13\frac{1}{2}$ per cent. They are appealing on the grounds that the belts should pay no tax 'like any other safety equipment'.

Henry Fielding in the *Sun*

A brown snake bit reptile-collector Neville Burns, 19, in Sydney yesterday – and dropped dead.

The People

Who notices by-lines? Only other journalists, say the cynics. And late-duty subs swapping notes in the Press Club. The American magazine *Holiday* has been casting an appraising eye over some of the off-beat by-lines which appear in the *New York Times*.

What newspaper in the world, it asks, can compete with such esoteric by-lines as Homer Bogart, Tad Szulc, Peter Kihss, Harry V. Fogeron, Peter Grose, Herbert Koshetz, Juan De Onis, Stacey V. Jones, Craig Claiborne, John Noble Witford, Dana Adams Schmidt, Edith Evand Asbury, Sam Pope Brewer, Benjamin Welles and Emanual Perlmutter.

The author of the *Holiday* article, Constantine Poulos (how's that for a by-line?), answers his own question: 'The most picturesque and possibly the most fascinating newspaper by-line in the world today appears in the *Sunday Telegraph*'.

You guessed, it's Peregrine Worsthorne. Mr Poulos considers this the 'most sublime, unbelievable name in the world'.

UK Press Gazette

Zoologists could only visit the hot springs in El Hamma with the permission of the local Kaliphat and with an escort of police, since it is reserved for the exclusive use of Muslim women bathers. An attempt was made to bring back a number of specimens alive in vacuum flasks so that further investigation could be carried out in Oxford.

Illustrated London News

To repair damaged tablecloths, first lay the tablecloth flat, with the hole uppermost.

Dublin Evening Mail

(As the earlier collections have made clear, Gobfrey Shrdlu is a past master in the use of metaphor: 'He had been wielding a double-edged sword in the shape of a boomerang that would come home to plague him and beat him by a large majority'; 'It is but the thin end of a white elephant', and so on. Below are two more examples of Shrdlu's literary genius. – D.P.)

It is the new magistrates who have broken the ice, and the supporters of both camps are curiously watching to see if they will find themselves in hot water.

Liverpool Echo

This criticism is not open, as Britishers would be, and consequently is difficult to nail down, but, like a snake in the grass, is whispering behind a hand which covers a sneering face.

Letter in *Rugeley Mercury*

SYDNEY, Friday

NURSING sister Patricia Gregan had six double Scotches at a hotel and missed her train home. So she went by goods train – riding 30 miles perched astride the couplings between two trucks. Part of the ride was through a mile and a half long tunnel.

Today in a Sydney court 54-year-old Mrs Gregan was charged with travelling on a portion of a goods train not intended for passengers and with being on railway property while intoxicated. She admitted both offences and was fined £27.

Mrs Gregan said: 'It was a very terrifying experience'. She promised she would not do it again.

Daily Mail

A husband disobeyed a court order not to molest his wife by leaving 150 embarrassing notes on her car and pouring a pint of beer and the contents of an ashtray over her head, said her counsel, Mr J. R. T. Rylance in the London Divorce Court today.

Lincolnshire Echo

District Attorney F. T. Graham, of Bronsville, Texas, got himself sent to jail for drunken driving this weekend. He became both prosecutor and defendant in a court case that followed his arrest after his car hit a dividing strip in the middle of a road last week.

When he was taken to police headquarters, Mr Graham signed a complaint against himself. In a special hearing he pleaded guilty to driving while intoxicated when his own charge against himself was read. He was fined $50 (£20 16s 8d) and sentenced to ten days' imprisonment. In the accident, the two left tyres of his car blew out, but he was unhurt.

The Daily Telegraph

The bride was attired in a navy blue georgette and hat to match, and carried a bouquet of roses and baby.

Mount Vernon (Iowa) *Telegraph*

The nearest hotel is over five miles away in one direction and practically twelve miles in the opposite direction.

Ulster Magazine and Eire Review

As a result of the incident many of the busts leaving Uxbridge Terminus are being followed by police cars.

Hayes Chronicle

```
THE TYPISTS' REPRODUCTION
EQUIPMENT IS NOT TO BE
INTERFERED WITH WITHOUT
THE PRIOR PERMISSION
OF THE MANAGER
```

Notice taped on photocopying machine

A man who had lost his right leg in 1946 bought eighteen pairs of shoes in the next twenty years – and never used the left ones.

Reveille

This woman walked very close to me, and it was obvious that underneath her clothing she wore little or nothing.

Sun

An inquest is to be held at Cranbrook on Wednesday into the death of 28-year-old Michael Morris, who was found with stab wounds at Paddock Wood on Friday night. Police said they were satisfied there were no suspicious circumstances attached to the man's death.

Kent & Sussex Courier

Assistants at a Romford, Essex, shop selling cooked breasts of chicken have been told by the management: 'Don't call them breasts. Say white meat.'

Sunday Mirror

A LETTER from the Ministry office asked: 'Is it necessary for your employees to climb a six-foot, glass-topped wall to get to work?'

Works manager Mr Terry Burrows thought the question amusing. So he replied: 'The normal mode of entry for employees is by using the springboard provided, bouncing over the mill surround, climbing the outside of Dixon's (285 ft) chimney, and descending inside the chimney and entering their place of work via the boiler house'. Mr Burrows, works manager at the Robert Todd yarn-spinning mill at Carlisle, ended his letter to the Department of Social Security: 'Ask a silly question . . .'

The letter was sourly received at the department's offices in Carlisle. An official said: 'Proper enquiries were instituted and there was no need for anyone to be flippant'. The department's query was over an injury claim by an employee who injured his foot climbing the wall to get to work. The worker was taking a short cut.

In Whitehall, the Department of Social Security said: 'Speaking generally, the success of such a claim would depend on whether it was necessary for workers to climb the wall to get to work, and whether such a practice was prohibited by the firm. Every case is judged on its merits.'

Daily Mail

Her dark hair is attractively set, and she has fine fair skin, which, she admits ruefully, comes out 'in a mass of freckles' at the first hint of sin.

Essex County Standard

Staff should empty the tea-pot and then stand upside down on the tea tray.

Office notice

GOD is Always At Hand To Help in Adversity. Please write Box 3092.

Border Counties Advertiser

When Miss Dixie Janice Byram, daughter of Mr and Mrs R. C. Byram of this city, became the bride of Edward Hersey on Friday afternoon at 2 o'clock at many friends here occurred last overshirt of lace. Her hat was the First Presbyterian Church.

Winter Haven (Florida) *Herald*

Police disbelieve a naval stoker who says he is not dead.

Essex paper

The editor wishes to thank the Rector for his kind help in editing this issue during her absence, and apologizes for its shortcomings on that account.

Parish magazine

GUIDED TOURS

Sight-seeing days for the public are being arranged by Godstone, Surrey, rural council for Lingfield's new sewage disposal works which are to be opened with a buffet lunch.

The Guardian

A MONKEY trained to pick coconuts jumped on to a man passing a coconut tree in Kuala Lumpur. He mistook his head for a nut and tried to twist it off. The man was taken to hospital with a strained neck.

Sunday Mirror

COLD SEX FOR TEA

HOUSEWIFE Mrs Rose C— bought an ice cream gâteau for tea at a village shop. When she opened the box at home in Duxford, near Cambridge, SEX stared her in the face – in large white letters across the top of the gateau.

Mrs C— asked the makers, T. Wall and Sons for an explanation. They apologized, gave her another gâteau and told her that the letters had been put there in a fit of pique by a worker who had been sacked.

Daily Mail

If you drive your car on to a policeman's foot – and don't remove it when he asks you to, are you guilty of assault? Three High Court judges yesterday disagreed on the answer to the question.

The Times

A woman, hit in the chest by a stray bullet, was rushed to a Saigon hospital. A nurse unclipped the woman's bra and – the bullet fell from its padding.

Sunday Mirror

Chief Detective T. G. Jackson told the Court that Smith was employed as a carter, and while taking a load of rubbish away had stolen the varnish. Prior to this there had been no stain against his character.

New Zealand paper

CHALLENGE! We believe that Michael Harvey, author of 1,500 short stories, is the prolific story writer of all time. If any other writer, living or dead, has equalled this record we shall be pleased to hear from him.

Advert in *World's Press News*

As for this puzzler: 'Was it he you were talking to' or 'Was it him you were talking to' Mr Lewis says the correct sentence would be: 'Was it he to whom you can also say it was she I were talking'. However, he adds, was thinking about.

Pittsburgh Press

Two priests, one of them the uncle of the bride, travelled from opposite ends of Miss Virginia Hinglass to Mr Bernard McInnes in Dublin yesterday.

Dublin *Sunday Independent*

I never went through that ghastly adolescent phase most girls experience. I went from child to woman in one go. One day I was a child. The next, a man.

News of the World

Mrs Margaret Wilson abandoned her driving test in mid-stream yesterday. Her examiner was in full agreement with the decision. After all, when you *are* in mid-stream it's the only thing to do.

Fortunately they managed to attract the attention of a passing driver – Mr Roger Goodman, who happened to be sailing up the River Wey at Guildford, Surrey, at the same time. Mrs Wilson and the Ministry of Transport examiner, Mr Victor Johnson, were sitting on top of the car – a Hillman Hunter belonging to Mrs Wilson's husband – when the motor-cruiser hove into sight.

Mr Goodman, a local councillor, said yesterday: 'I was flabbergasted. I came round a bend and saw the car in the middle of the river with two people sitting on the roof as it went down. I slowed down and went alongside and my wife threw a lifebelt to the woman who said she couldn't swim. We got her into the boat and the driving examiner crawled across the roof. We took them across to the bank and the police had already arrived.'

Mrs Wilson had just turned sharp left into the ominously named Riverside Road when things began to take a turn for the worse. 'This was my fifth test and it had been going much better than the previous four,' she said at her home last night. 'I'd just gone round the corner in first gear on full lock. I said to myself: "I'm too close to the edge", and then I must have put my foot on the accelerator instead of the brake because I went straight through the railings into the river. The car started to sink. I had my window open and got on to the seat and half out. The examiner opened his door and the water rushed in. Then he got out of the window.'

Mr Johnson, a senior examiner, was sent home 'in a state of shock'. But, in accordance with proper procedure, he did manage to hang on to his briefcase and clip-board during his flight to safety. Which was probably just as well. For a Ministry of Transport official said: 'As this was a terminated test, we cannot say whether the lady passed or failed until the examiner makes his report'.

Daily Mail

As soon as Miss Walker knew she was to sin, she telephoned her husband in Kansas.

New York Times

La orquesta ejecutó el 'Good sabe the Queen', coreado por la concurencia, lo mismo que el 'Forisa Folley good fillow'.

La Nacion, Buenos Aires

Douglas Orville Miles (20), student, pleaded not guilty to having an offensive weapon (two 4-inch nails) and pleaded not builty to using insulting stomach of another man in the behaviour.

Yorkshire Evening Post

The after-lunch talk was given by Mr Derek Wigram – school headmaster retired, but now serving the Lord in an advisory capacity.

Crusade

The order governing the purchase of Corporation houses could not be varied at this stage – the obvious thing to do was to form a new scheme for the purchase of dress with matching hat.

Sligo Champion

DOVER ROAD. Semi-det. house with sea through lounge.

Folkestone, Hythe and District Herald

WIFE SWOPS CHILD FOR RECORD-PLAYER

Mr and Mrs Arthur Blank swopped their two-year-old daughter Jacqueline for a secondhand record-player. Three days later they sold the record-player for £3 because it didn't work.

Now Mrs Blank, 24, wants to buy another radiogram and get back little Jacqueline. She said yesterday: 'It was quite a wrench parting with Jackie. But we have a little girl of seven months and I am expecting another baby in February. Arthur had had his eye on the record-player for some time. He had even offered £15 for it. When Jackie was suggested instead it seemed quite fair.'

Daily Mail

A general practitioner colleague is related to have somersaulted his car end to end twice. Incredibly alive and unscathed he staggered over to a nearby cottage where he knew he could ring the garage. The good lady was just putting down the phone. 'Oh Doctor, I've only just called your house. How good of you to come so quickly. There's been a terrible accident outside.'

Rural Medicine

He said the car came out of the car park at about 10 mph, straight at him. 'It was very close and I was frightened,' he told the jury. 'I thought it was going to hit me. Then it turned to the right. I said "You silly bastard" to the driver.'

He said an elderly man got out of the front passenger seat, took him by the shoulders and told him not to swear. This caused three tins of dog food which he had inside his shirt to start falling out. He took the tins out and put them on the bridge parapet behind him. As he did so the driver came up and hit him in the eye.

Western Gazette

T–C

Captain Thompson said that the epidemic of laryngitis among men might be traced to the development of central heating in London hotels and restaurants and the scantiness of women's attire.

Kent paper

This policy offers absolute security in the event of any kind of fatal accident.

Insurance advert

In last night's performance of *The Gondoliers*, Mr Robertson, as the Grand Inquisitor, might have been a gentleman in reality, so ably did he fill the part.

Provincial paper

ERRORS. No responsibility can be accepted for losses arising from typographical errors. Advertisers are expected to check their smalls to ensure correct appearance.

Rhodesia Herald

WORKING COOK-HOUSEKEEPER required by professional man and own self-contained bed-sitting wife.

Advert in *The Daily Telegraph*

This Appliance will reduce
your hips, or bust.

Advert in *People's Home Journal*

A Chesham shopkeeper admitted in court last Wednesday that a piece of pie which was said to be unfit for human consumption was from an old batch. She maintained that she had not meant to sell it and that it was intended for her husband's tea.

Bucks Examiner

Dustman Terry Holman yesterday admitted stealing bananas from a supermarket by hooking them with a wire and pulling them one by one through the letter-box. Holman, 31, of Station Road, Wombourne, Staffordshire, was fined £5 at Wolverhampton.

Daily Mail

MAN BITES HORSE!

Daily Sketch headline

This potter is also thought to have made the cow milk-jugs, in which the tail of the animal forms a handle and the mild pours disturbingly from its open mouth.

Birmingham Post

The second visit of the Welsh National Opera Company to Liverpool opens at the Royal Court on November 3rd. They will also give Verdi's *Macbeth* in which Lady Macbeth is played by the Lancashire singer Pauline Tinsley and Boris Godunov by Mussourgsky.

Liverpool Daily Post

The customs search was continued when the ship arrived at Tilbury – and the half-ounce of drug was found by a specially trained dog hidden in a hose-reel.

Oldham Evening Chronicle

Mr O. R. Wise stated that the whole of the racing fraternity of the Dominion were prepared to stand behind the Minister, provided he stood behind them.

New Zealand paper

A Grand Jury in Los Angeles have indicted welterweight boxer Art Aragon on a charge of offering a bride to an opponent.

Bradford Telegraph and Argus

GENTLEMAN desires genuine
friendship of unattached lady, 40–
45, any reply answered confidently.

Reading Chronicle

(My favourite Shrdlu items are those which give scope for endless speculation, such as these: 'Old-established manu-facturer of suspension bridges seeks door-to-door salesman', 'Apologies to patrons for inconvenience last Sunday night owing to bust mishap', and 'GRAPEFRUIT LATE TELLING POLICE OF INJURED MAN'. Below is one which got me so intrigued that I wrote to the advertiser for elucidation. No reply! – D.P.)

MISLAID, l'Etacq area. Live limpets marked 5, 6, 11, 14. Information to 'J.E.P.', Box 670, gratefully received.

Advert in *Jersey Evening Post*

In his life, Jacobus van Dyn's contribution to society has been dubious in the extreme. He has been a bootlegger and a gunman for Al Capone. In his death he will leave behind a macabre memento – the skin of his bald, tattooed head. He has sold it to a Woolwich tattooist Jack Ringo.

Whenever 71-year-old Jacobus is short of money, Mr Ringo helps him out. He has already given him about £50. Mr Ringo will collect on his investment when Jacobus dies. The skin will be taken from his head, preserved, and displayed in Mr Ringo's shop at a small fee for charity.

The whole of Jacobus's body is adorned with tattoos. But he is especially proud of the tattoos on his bald head. They include the signs of the Zodiac and various 'way out' patterns. Most people will find Jacobus's £50 deal macabre in the extreme. But if you *should* want to view the tattoos on his skull and face, don't wait until he dies. If you go to Speakers' Corner, Hyde Park, you will usually find Jacobus, speaking on most subjects. And, if you are tall enough, you can see the tattoos for free.

The People

The first hearing was adjourned to enable the students to be regally represented.

Surrey Advertiser

Salt Lake City (AP) – Saying military nerve gas was not the cause of a massive Utah sheep kill last spring, an Army commander announced on Friday a plan to keep it from happening again.

Springfield (Montana) *Daily News*

It is time the law stepped in to prohibit people who have no more sense than to make their dogs follow them on bicycles, especially at night.

Letter in *Leicester Mercury*

One main event in London was Cruft's Dog Show. For two days dogs and dog-owners from all over the country crowded the huge halls and galleries, barking at one another in fierce competition.

Aberdeen Press and Journal

He said the printer had 'read off the wrong line', but promised that arrangements were already in hadn ot hvae tch netx editoin pirnted korrectly.

Saturday Telegraph

Midwife Maria Sack asks us to say that neither she nor her husband is identical with the Frau Sack who was arrested in Schönberg.

, *Berliner Tageblatt*

After negligence had been denied by her employers, a 50-year-old café manageress whose big toe was broken when a 7-lb block of frozen cod fell on it, had her claim for damages dismissed yesterday. She was Diana M— of Arthur Road, Rotherham.

Yorkshire Post

HUSBAND WORE ENGAGEMENT RING ON HIS TOE

Thomas Wallace had lots of obsessions. One was about his wife's engagement ring. Mr Wallace felt that his wife, Joan, was careless about looking after the ring. And when he found it lying around one day, he decided to teach her a lesson. He picked up the ring and popped it on one of his toes . . . and waited.

Mrs Wallace thought she had lost the ring. She feared that her husband would be furious. For a time she did not see the ring on her husband's toe because he wore two pairs of socks – and only took off one pair at night. But, a Divorce Court judge said yesterday, Mrs Wallace eventually persuaded her husband to take off both pairs of socks, for darning or washing. And there, on his toe, she saw the 'lost' engagement ring.

That – Mr Justice Cumming-Bruce said – was one of the many examples of Mr Wallace's 'lamentable and wanton lack of consideration' for his wife's feelings. When the couple married in 1963, the bride was infatuated with Mr Wallace, the judge said. But the husband's conduct – including 'odd behaviour' at the register office – soon broke down her eagerness to please.

When Mrs Wallace became pregnant, her husband tried to make her eat bone-meal fertilizer – thinking it would cut the risk of calcium deficiency. Mrs Wallace refused. Mr Wallace tasted the fertilizer himself and dropped the idea. The marriage ended when Mrs Wallace left home because she found that her husband was planning to take in a lodger. Mrs Wallace was granted a decree nisi on the ground of cruelty.

Daily Mirror

Stenographer – five years legal
experience, seeks permanent con-
nexions. Late 1967 model, good
shape, many extras, used for pleasure spins by private owners. A real
bargain. 522 E. Broad St.

Cleveland (Ohio) *News*

Mr Thornbury was born in Victoria and immediately
entered the engineering profession.

Vancouver paper

The police are trying to trace the relatives of a four months
old baby found on a doorstep. It was dressed in clothing of
very poor quality, and had been much laundered.

Surrey paper

Under the baton of Mr S. Rutherford the Cosmopolitan
Club orchestra provided musical numbers. Miss Maisie
Ringell's outstanding features convulsed the audience.

Gisborne Herald

From Llandridnod you proceed along the lovely valley of the
Ithon, growing more beautiful as you proceed.

Motor Cycle

A new golf club has opened in Kenya. A course rule says that if your ball lands on or by a crocodile you have the option of moving the ball a club's length away – or moving the crocodile.

Sun

NIMES: Exasperated by the time she waited for the telephone operator to answer, Madame Gilberte Rivet, 45, of Bagnols-sur-Ceze, near Nimes, stormed round to the exchange. There she beat up Madame Josette Conil, the operator on duty, and the police had to be called to break up the fight. Now Madame Gilberte faces charges of causing grievous bodily harm.

Evening Standard

From the Reverend W. A. Tighe

Sir, Aeroplanists should keep their eyes skinned for agents other than human at the earth-end of the kite string. I have seen a horse flying a kite.

It was in Hongkong twenty years ago. The kite swooped into a paddock where horses grazed: the string snapped, leaving perhaps 30 feet of its length still attached to the framework: the free end fell across the rump of a horse: a twitch of the tail secured (mysteriously) the string: the animal moved, felt the drag, moved faster, became frightened, began to gallop – and the kite rose and soared beautifully and in partnership with its flier round and round the paddock for almost a minute.

Three others saw this with me; they are all alive today. For the benefit of the unkindly suspicious, this equine feat was observed during the last of three hard sets of tennis and more than two hours after a very light lunch.

Yours truthfully, WILFRED A. TIGHE

Letter in *The Times*

Gardeners should waste no time. Tie your pants in now before the south-easters blow.

Advert in Cape paper

Billingsgate is up in arms, and should the project be persisted in, it is feared that an sgOugo wsRcoastpk shrdlu shrdlshrdlshrdlshrdlhrdlu outburst of language may ensue such as this country has never yet heard.

Dublin Evening Mail

The book contains a portrait of the author and several other quaint illustrations.

Liverpool paper

Henry VIII by his own efforts increased the population of England by 40,000.

Northern San Diego Shoppers' Guide

Copy typists require work at home. Anything awful considered.

Rochdale Observer

The Bishop of Lichfield will conduct the baptismal service at St Chad's Church next Sunday morning at eleven o'clock. To READERS, You will assist *The Mercury* and the district generally by patronizing our advertisers whenever possible.

Lichfield Mercury

Fish with large stomach ulcers which have been caught off the south coast may have got their ailment by swallowing plastic beakers thrown off Channel ferries.

The Guardian

GNANASAMUNTHAMURTHI NAICKER intends to change his name to Gnanasamunthamurthi Moodley, reports the Government Gazette in Durban.

The Evening News

REWARD for any information concerning a small tan & white short haired terrier, taken from my yard sometime Tuesday. This dog answers to name of Patches and is very old and stone deaf. 229 Goetting Way.

Advert in *Vista Press* (California)

When my husband reads in bed on warm nights he puts a collander over his head. He says it keeps off the flies, shades his eyes from the light and lets in air at the same time.

Letter in *Good Shopping* quoted in
New Statesman's 'This England' column

Miss O'Neill said Wardlow picked up an axe and struck her twice on the head with it. She was in bed at the time. Shortly afterwards, he hit her with a can of soup. 'He opened it then and we both had the soup,' she said.

Edinburgh Evening News

Heavy rains again fell in Khartoum and vicinity last Saturday night and several lakes have been formed in various parts of the town, some of which are still navigable. Mosquitos are not allowed to breed in them, under penalty of a heavy fine.

Egyptian Mail

John Cardew stated that he had seen a large number of skulls thrown up during an interment. He did not think that was a proper thing. He would cry his eyes out if he saw it done to his own.

Irish Times

Strawberries, which by now should be well in season, are unripened on the damp ground. Already many growers are getting covered with a grey mould.

Manchester Evening Post

Erection of the bride over the level crossing at Beeston Station will cost £135,300 8s 2d.

Stapleford and Sandiacre News

Madrid proposes to utilize the water brought to the city by an old camel to produce about three thousand electrical horse-power.

Montreal Gazette

MRS VICKERY GETS A STEAM-ROLLER
FOR HER BIRTHDAY

HOUSEWIFE Mrs Betty Vickery went for a driving lesson yesterday – on a six-ton steam-roller. Mother-of-four Mrs Vickery was given the 1907 Aveling and Porter road roller as a surprise birthday present by her husband, garage owner Mr Alan Vickery.

Now she's practising 'like mad' for her test so that she can drive it to traction engine rallies. Steam-rollers run in the family. Her father, Mr Frank Pratley, 73, earned his living for almost 50 years driving them. He took her for her lesson yesterday – a 5 mph trip down the High Street at Harpenden, Hertfordshire.

At home in Snatchup, Redbourn, Hertfordshire, Mrs Vickery, 32, said: 'It takes an hour to work up steam and 1 cwt of coal lasts only five miles'. Mr Vickery said: 'I spotted the steam-roller at a garage at High Wycombe, in Buckingham-shire, and I realized it would be just the thing for my wife'.

Daily Mail

There were murmurs of disapproval from a de-fence solicitor. Mr Peter Smith, prosecuting for Havering Council, rose to inform puzzled magis-trates: 'I think my friend is disturbed because the witness has taken the oath on a steak and kidney pie'.

Hornchurch Echo

A *Phocaena phocaena* was found today propped up in one of the cubicles of the men's lavatory in Glasgow Central station. The staff thought it was a dolphin, but the 4 ft 64 lb carcass was identified as a porpoise by the museums' department at Kelvingrove Park. How it had come into the lavatory nobody knew: one gentleman said: 'We had heavy rain and there was flooding, but this is ridiculous'.

The Times

An interesting address on 'The National Care of the Child' by Miss Palmer was much appreciated by all, and Mrs Lever in a short address made an appeal for the use of the humane killer.

Berkshire paper

FLIES COMING INTO CONTACT WITH THIS PREPARATION OF DDT DIE WITHOUT HOPE OF RECOVERY

Label on bottle

Let us nip this political monkey business in the bud before it sticks to us like a leech.

Letter in San Francisco Chronicle

Inspector Jones said that the usual red herring of Mr Skinner's had been exploded – that there was a flat tyre.

Isle of Man paper

Even members of the Press have gone out of their way to rub in the biller pill.

Bristol paper

Today's hint tells you how to keep your hair in first-class order. Cut it out and paste it on a piece of cardboard and hang it in your bathroom.

Essex paper

Waitresses used eyebrow tweezers to remove flakes of rust in dishes of jelly at Bath's Pump Room. And Councillor Will Johns, who told this story to the city council last night, asked that in future the eyebrow tweezers should be sterilized.

Western Daily Press quoted in *New Statesman*

A 7-inch edible snail was caught at London Airport yesterday after it had hidden on a Comet from Nairobi and Benghazi. The snail was taken to the RSPCA hostel.

Daily Mail quoted in
New Stateman's 'This England' column

Nearly every night scrapmetal worker Derek Forbes took his young bride through a couple of rounds of boxing before they went to bed. Mr Forbes, 32, is keen on boxing. His 20-year-old wife, Nora is not. And she has not been feeling too well lately. Now – after three weeks of marriage – Mary is back home with mother. 'My husband doesn't want a wife, he wants a punch-bag,' she said yesterday.

The People quoted in *New Statesman*

Scotland Yard is searching for more space in which to store its embarassingly large stock of obscene books and pictures, and HM Customs is forbidden to burn any more obscene books because they were breaking the rules of a smokeless zone by making black smoke.

The Guardian

An 11-year-old boy used his glass eye and spare to play marbles. He broke both. He is to be given another eye under the Health Service.

Daily Mail

The marksmanship of the headquarters company is highly satisfactory and the shooting of the regimental sergeant-major was especially praiseworthy.

Daily Express

Alderman Johnston moved that, pending the passing of the street by-law, that all vehicles on Columbia Street be required to keep to the left going up and to the right going down.

The British Columbian

Letters were sent to 665 men. Each envelope was marked 'Important' in large letters, so that those men who could not read might ask to have the letters read to them.

American Education Digest

The Magistrate, Mr Edward Blank, was mounted on Saturday, with all the accuracy and timing of a military exercise.

Waltham Forest Express

Very Rev M. Canon D—, ugly and unsightly debris heap, was being transformed into a delightful miniature park.

Limerick Chronicle

There were no failures in the Scots' line up. The forwards fought for every ball and rampaged in the looc.

Evening Citizen, Glasgow

Under a notice offering 'Honey for Sale', James Thompson of The Caravan, Prairie Road, put up another which read: 'Ignore the Bald-headed Old Bath-bun Next Door'. At Stratford-on-Avon Petty Sessions on Friday, Thompson was fined £1 for displaying an advertisement without planning permission.

Evesham Journal

Recently I read with some envy that dentists are providing tanks of goldfish to soothe the nerves of patients. I am the wife of an overworked and underpaid general practitioner. I had several goldfish before the National Health Service descended upon us, but I had to serve these to my husband for supper one night.

Letter in *Sunday Express*

Crossed in love, Nicholas Ray, 20-year-old bank clerk of Needham Market, Suffolk, put on a top hat and frock coat and rode 85 miles to London on a penny-farthing bicycle.

He returned by train yesterday with the penny-farthing in the guard's van. He said: 'When I was jilted it made me feel an awful failure. The ride restored my confidence.'

Daily Express quoted in
New Statesman's 'This England' column

When Det Sgt Nichols asked 'What's the idea?' Harris replied: 'Everybody has his own peculiarities; this is mine'. He said he had been travelling naked in trains for about two years, but did not think anyone had seen him.

News of the World

Mrs Joe Sexton and children, of Deadwood Gulch, were guests of the A. Dennys family on Sunday.

Mrs Dennys is almost confined to her bed with nervous exhaustion.

Idaho paper

We make a speciality of gorillas and chimpanzees. They are wonderfully intelligent and can be trained right up to the human standard in all except speech. One of our directors, Mr Alec Jackson and his wife are both able to be tamed to live in captivity.

Irish paper

Winners in the home-made claret section were Mrs Davis (fruity, well-rounded), Mrs Rayner (fine colour and full-bodied), and Miss Ogle-Smith (slightly acid, but should improve if laid down).

From a Leicestershire parish magazine

Arthur already holds black belt grades in Judo and Karate, so this award makes him a leading marital arts practitioner in the Isle of Man.

Mona's Herald

He smiled and let his gaze fall to hers, so that her cheek began to glow. Ecstatically she waited until his mouth slowly neared her own. She knew only one thing: rdoeniadtrdgoveniardgoverdgovnrdgog.

Badische Presse

Since becoming pregnant I find that when my right foot itches I get a letter; when my left foot itches my husband gets a letter.

Letter in *Woman's Sunday Mirror*

THE FAMOUS

4 cup

BRA

Advert in a women's weekly

The Management Committee of K— Hospital chose to buy twelve plastic bedpans instead of the traditional stainless steel bedpans. Cost was the over-riding factor though humanitarian values also influenced their decision; plastic is warmer to the touch than steel. Plastic was unpopular with the staff as it has a tendency to stain.

The following compromise was achieved: patients, or the relatives of discharged patients, who wished to show their gratitude to the hospital and its staff would be encouraged to present memorial steel bedpans on whose sides the donor's name would be engraved.

Item quoted in *True Stories*
by Christopher Logue (Four Square, 1966)

Miss Georgina P. Mason, psychologist, quoted the case of a nine-year-old boy who ran amok with a hatchet in the large family of which he was a member, saying, 'There are far too many bairns here'. She showed how by psychological treatment he became completely adjusted and several years later was working a guillotine in a printer's establishment.

Ross-shire Journal

'The lack of toilet facilities is absolutely disgraceful,' he said. The only solution was a major reconstruction of the House or a new Chamber.

The Daily Telegraph

They shot under Hammersmith Bridge, their ears scooping away the water in unison.

Devon Evening Echo

The referrees must put the ball in the scrums but not necessarily be rolled along the ground.

New Zealand paper

The strike leaders had called a meeting that was to have been held in a bra near the factory, but it was found to be too small to hold them all.

South London Press

Police say the 7-inch picture, depicting a declining nude, had been stolen some time ago.

Straits Times

Miss Jennifer Walton was an art student. Usually she lived in London but sometimes she occupied premises in Hampshire. John Carter, a married man of thirty-five, came to the door of these premises, knocked, and when Miss Walton went to see who was there he explained that he was not feeling very well.

Miss Walton invited him in and brought a glass of water. While drinking the water Carter told Miss Walton that he was suffering from painter's colic. He finished the glass, lay down on the floor. and asked Miss Walton to stand on his stomach.

'The best cure is a weight on the stomach,' he said. Miss Walton stood on his stomach for a minute. 'He told me I wasn't heavy enough,' she said. 'I fetched a box but that wasn't heavy enough either.' Feeling that she had done everything in her power to help Carter, Miss Walton suggested that the large man who lived next door might bring express relief.

'A large woman would be preferable,' said Carter. 'I fetched Mrs Stone from next door,' Miss Walton continued, 'and we stood on his stomach together.' After this Carter felt better.

The Magistrate bound him over for twelve months.

News item quoted in *True Stories*
by Christopher Logue

Does Lady travelling home one night with bottle of sherry and Apocryphal Bible remember long conversation with travelling companion who hereby confesses with shame having advanced blasphemous theories, and has now bitterly repented of them?

Advert in *Brighton Evening Argus*

General practitioners were responsible for more than 80 per cent of the hospital confinements of borough mothers.

Report of a Medical Officer of Health

Mr John P— will play Macbeth. The Society hopes to make an interesting announcement concerning Lady Macbeth at an early date.

Statement by Amateur Drama Society

Among the first to enter was Mrs Clara Adams of Erie, Pa., lone woman passenger. Slowly her nose was turned around to face in a south-westerly direction away from the hangar doors. Then like some strange beast, she crawled along the grass.

California paper

FRIENDS' ACADEMY, Locust Valley, Long Island, Co-educational, with special opportunities for boys.

Friend's Intelligencer

It is announced that the Consuls have requested the setting apart of a neutral zone two square millimetres in extent, within which foreigners may take up their quarters.

Birmingham Daily Post

Mr Len Stanley, who was ordered by a county court judge to fill in the hole he dug across a country lane near his home in Dorset, has done so. But now another hole has appeared – dug by his father, Mr Fred Stanley, aged 78. He said: 'The judge didn't say I couldn't dig one of my own'.

The Guardian

As an old age pensioner, I wish to draw the attention of elderly readers to the dangers of the tricycle.

The other day I stepped off my doorstep and two racing tricyclists came hurling upon me. But for my startled cry of horror I am sure I would have been knocked to the ground.

Recently I have seen children riding tricycles crawl behind old ladies and deliberately batter their calves. The hurt cries of the victims have caused fiendish chuckles from the children.

Letter in *Manchester Evening News*

SOUTHPORT
A TOWN OF OLD PEOPLE
One in six over 65
GRAVE PROBLEM

Liverpool Echo and Evening Express

Introducing the guest of honour the Mayor explained that the reason Father Christmas had not arrived earlier in the festive season was that the Town Council had inadvertently sent the cesspool emptier to meet him instead of a lorry.

Wisbech Standard quoted in
New Statesman's 'This England' column

Detached private hotel, excellently situated near Torquay Sea Front. Practically on the level.

Devonshire paper

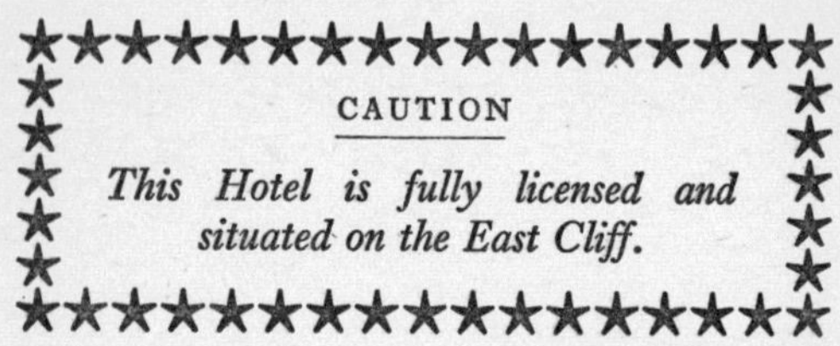

Bournemouth hotel brochure

Remember a Snooks & Co ladder will last twenty years or more if you don't wear out the rungs with use.

From a leaflet

For some time past running water has been installed at the cemetery to the satisfaction of the inhabitants.

Républicain Lorrain

Princess Margaret's daring but very fashionable hat caused a sensation when she opened a school for the blind at Sevenoaks.

France-Soir

Last night a Glasgow woman bought a pie, and on eating a portion of it later felt something stick in her throat. She then pulled an elastic garter from her mouth.

On taking the pie back to the shop her money was refunded.

Glasgow Evening Times

Gent, quiet, reserved, would like to meet gent.

Advert in *Yorkshire Evening Post*

I'm sure numerous readers of the *Echo* would get quite a kick last Friday night on reading about the four-inch caterpillar sent to you from Birkenhead, plus the four-foot jellyfish found on Prestatyn shore.

News of this nature stirs the imagination, and helps to counteract the depressing news about the crisis.

Letter in *Liverpool Echo*

The Vicar of H— thinks it impossible for his parishioners – most are boarding-house keepers – to keep all the Ten Commandments, so he has reduced them to nine for his services.

Evening Standard quoted in *New Statesman*

Los Angeles Municipal Court Judge Richard Amerian found the plea of innocent to a charge of parking next to a fire hydrant hard to believe. The accused, Maurice Kleinman, aged 19, told the judge: 'The fire hydrant parked next to me . . .'

A check showed that the City Works Department had indeed installed the equipment AFTER Kleinman had parked his car.

Daily Express

(The five items below are translated from *La Réalité Dépasse La Fiction* by Albert Aycard and Jacqueline Franck.)

Grease stains on furniture may be removed with alkali, but old stains, being difficult to remove, must be tackled as soon as they are made.

Dauphiné-Libéré

The Italian doctor looked at me fixedly above his plate of ravioli and tomato and his smile displayed thirty-two artistically aligned molars.

Touring-Club

We have promised to help the elderly as much as we can; we have begun to put our promises into effect. Food in school canteens has been improved.

Bulletin municipal d'Aubervilliers

Yes, Simone killed her husband, but she acted alone said the latter, a local café owner.

L'Aurore

Widower wishes to correspond with lady of 60 to 68 years old with a view to marriage and able to milk a cow.

Echo Républicain de la Beauce et du Perche

TROOPS WATCH
ORANGE MARCH

Headline in The Daily Telegraph

Thirty-six-year-old Alexander Marshall, Portland dockyard crane driver who pulled three railway trucks with his teeth, wants to pull a motor coach along Piccadilly with his hair. He is applying to the Metropolitan Police for permission to do it at Whitsun.

Sunday Express

I myself was in charge of such a gasworks near Norwich some years ago where on a Sunday morning I would take my armchair on to the top of the gas-holder and read the newspaper – my weight giving just the extra pressure needed to cook the dinners (a reduction of pressure was unheard of then of course, but it would have been very easy to apply).

Letter in The Times

Mr James Cooper, a butcher, described seeing on September 23rd this year a large monkey 'which was as big as an adult and resembled a chimpanzee', sitting in the defendant's shop window.
It devoured twelve packets of Keating's beetle powders and eight packets of Bob Martin's powders one by one, and then disappeared.

Berrow's Worcester Journal

Middlewich Housing and Open Spaces Committee had a seat placed at the junction of Kitfield Avenue and Booth Lane, but as complaints have been received of persons using the seat also using bad language, the seat is to be moved to another point on the same site.

Northwich Guardian

Madame Quillet's assassin, after striking her, had strangled his victim with blows from a hatchet.

Parisien libéré

LONDONDERRY Development Commission has plans to spend about £24,000 within the next few months on improving the standard of street fighting in the city centre and a number of housing estates.

Belfast Telegraph

GREAT YARMOUTH. Comfortable apartments. Five minutes from the sea. Germs moderate.

Advert in *Railway Magazine*

Golf, tennis, bowls, riding, sailing, fishing, indoor amusements and night porter completes the ideal holiday.

Advert in St Ives guide book

If you're in a cinema, put your arm round her and don't be bashful. All the people around you are doing the same.

Letter in *Sunday Pictorial*

The Archbishop scouted the idea that the work of the ministry was to engage in the social amenities of the afternoon tea-table. It offered a real man's job to the youth of the Church today. Afternoon tea was served as usual.

Diocesan magazine

'I don't know whether I am the father of the child. I am only an apprentice,' wrote a man to the Woking Bench in answer to a summons against him for an affiliation order.

Woking Herald

The greatest shock to the magazine reader will be the assertion that wolves do not run in packs. He might be willing to grant that much else in lupine lore is untrue, but 'everybody knows' that wolves run in packs. One might as well deny that sheep graze in herds! Yet men who have had to do with wolves over periods of years do deny it.

Stefansson, who has seen thousands of wolves in their natural state, says that he has never seen a pack of wolves – has never seen, that is, any aggregate of wolves in close association larger than the parents and cubs of one family. For more than twenty years he has amused himself by tracking down all accounts of wolf packs that have come to his attention, and not one has been authenticated to his satisfaction. He is convinced that wolf 'packs' are a vulgar error, and Dr E. W. Nelson, former Chief of the United States Biological Survey, who joined him in the chase, shares his conviction.

So it is also with all accounts of wolves attacking people – young or old, brides, grooms, trappers, soldiers, Russians, Turks, or air-mail pilots. There is no authenticated record of any human beings being attacked and eaten by a wolf. For years the Biological Survey in Washington investigated every published account of the killing of human beings by wolves in the United States or in Canada, 'and without a single exception they proved to be purely imaginary'. The unromantic fact seems to be that wolves, though (like many other animals) extremely curious, are also extremely cautious.

The Natural History of Nonsense
by Bergen Evans (Michael Joseph, 1947)

JUST OUT. Revised and enlarged RULES OF PUNCTION. A valuable, easy-to-understand text for secretaries, writers, and students. For a free copy send a stamped self-addressed envelope. Ask for PUNCIATION pamphlet.

Indiana paper

One collapsible baby, good condition, $7.

Advert in Canadian paper

At St Peter's Church on Friday, the Vicar, on examining the offertory box, found that the church had been abstracted.

Bedford paper

The tendency of merchandise offices to restrict buying generally has found some stores very short of corsets – a department which consistently maintained figures throughout the past months.

Draper's Record

It was a sort of Daniel and Goliath battle, in which the stronger and bigger man always appeared to hold the mastery.

Scottish paper

To let – young girl two storeys, beautiful balcony, central heating, moderate rent.

L'Alsace

A MIXED PEDIGREE

Joseph Bloggs: 'I can't follow it, my dear boy. It makes me dizzy!'

John Snoggs: 'It's very simple. Listen again! You happen to be my father's brother-in-law, my brother's father-in-law, and also my father-in-law's brother. You see, my father was—.'

But Mr Bloggs refused to hear any more. Can the reader show how this extraordinary triple relationship might have come about?

No 55 in H. E. Dudeney's
Amusements in Mathematics

SOLUTION

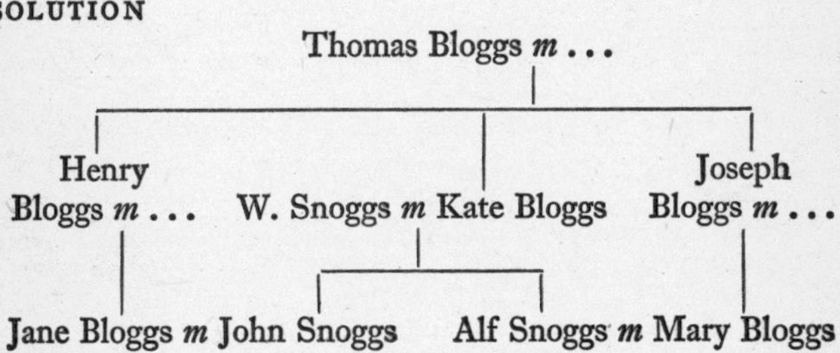

The letter *m* stands for 'married'. It will be seen that John Snoggs can say to Joseph Bloggs, 'You are my *father's brother-in-law*, because my father married your sister Kate; you are my *brother's father-in-law* because my brother Alfred married your daughter Mary; and you are my *father-in-law's brother*, because my wife Jane was your brother Henry's daughter'.

Sight of ants carrying tomato skins inspired members of a Stafford Nature Society to move a boulder, weighing two and a half tons, half a mile up Pudding Hill.

Reynolds' News

She took off her shoes and I undid the laces of mine. A good warm smell already enveloped us; the restaurant was becoming enticing.

Elle

The special consignments at Jacksons Ltd of Bromley this week are salmon, live lobsters, whitebait, and Marche Héroique in D flat.

Bromley District Times

In America it is true that our general rules of evidence and principles of law are mainly followed, and there is very little danger of an innocent man being acquitted.

The Globe

PUBLIC HEALTH PROBLEM

———

Special Committee to sit on bed bug

Liverpool paper

Next to the fact that it hides its head in the sand, the best-known thing about the ostrich is that it can digest iron . . . The extent of this belief and the harm that it causes is almost incredible. There is probably not a menagerie in existence that has not lost several birds in consequence of their being fed nail files and other lethal tit-bits by zoo-haunting zanies.

Mr E. G. Boulenger, for many years a director of the London Zoological Society, lists the post-mortem findings in an ostrich that had died a few days after a holiday had burdened the zoo with an unusually large number of clodpolls. From the organs of the unhappy bird were extracted 'two handkerchiefs, three gloves, a Kodak film spool, three feet of thick string, a pencil, a part of a celluloid comb, a bicycle tyre valve, an alarm clock winding key, a glove fastener, a piece of wood five inches long, part of a rolled gold necklace, two collar studs, a penny, four halfpennies, two farthings, and a Belgian franc piece' – a collection which is now on exhibition in the museum of the Tropical School of Medicine.

The Natural History of Nonsense
by Bergen Evans

We are asked to state that Miss Butler did not stroke the cow which tossed her. It was some distance from her at first, but after she had said 'Good morning' to it, the animal rushed at her.

Hertfordshire Pictorial

Indicating how thoroughly they did their job, he told the Council that, at their last meeting, all the members of the committee were engaged, for a time, on counting sheets of toilet paper to see which firm offered the best value.

Lincolnshire Echo

T–D

We have the sad duty to inform you of the death of M. Giovanni, recalled to God by accident.

Paris-Normandie

The Red Cross paid for emergency care and later found a free bed for him in an institution specializing in the treatment of artcritics.

Arizona Star

The dispensary, however, will be open in the afternoon from one-thirty to four on Monday to Friday for decapitated students with the nurse in charge.

Pomona College Student Life

WOMAN KICKED BY HER HUSBAND SAID TO BE GREATLY IMPROVED

Headline in Illinois paper

Two cycles belonging to girls that had been left leaning against lamp-posts were badly damaged.

Glasgow paper

Mr A. Asprey, of the famous firm of silver and gold smiths, talked about quality in his craft. One of the examples he brought along was a gold nail file covered with crushed diamonds to give it an extra fine filing action. 'It's a great economy,' he assured me, 'for although it costs £140 it will never wear out.'

Scotsman quoted in
New Statesman's 'This England' column

Today is Daisy's, the Pekinese's, sixth birthday, and she wishes to send her love to all mankind.

Advert in *The Times*

A Portsmouth man believes he has found the way to talk to hedgehogs – although he does not know the meaning of what he says to them.

The Evening News

A St Albans motorist, summoned at St Albans Divisional Sessions, on Saturday for a driving offence, was asked by a police Inspector: 'After the accident, why did you raise your bowler hat to acknowledge the driver of the other car involved, when you did not know him?'

The motorist replied: 'The accident had caused the hat to become crammed down over my eyes and ears and – although it might have been polite to raise it to the other driver – I lifted it to alleviate my discomfort'.

Herts Advertiser

American Electric Blanket for sale, new. Owner leaving. Rosepink colour.

Advert in Sunday paper

Carr was given out leg before, as he appeared likely to make a good score.

Report of village cricket match

You really have seen only half the show if you see the Paris imports worn on the mannequins alone. There is almost double the excitement in looking under and inside the clothes.

Women's Wear Daily

Dyke stated in his complaint that the defendant owned a large dog that walked the floor most of the night, held noisy midnight parties, and played a radio so that sleep was impossible.

Australian paper

CAPITAL PET ANIMAL HOSPITAL
Dogs called for, fleas removed and returned to you for $1.00.

Advert in Washington paper

The bride wore an ivory georgette dress with a Brussels net veil. The bridegroom wore the DSO.

South London paper

I am going hunting and wish to take my gun with me on the train. The ticket agent tells me I may not take it on the coach, while the baggage man will not take it because of its excessive length (1.7 yards), since he is forbidden to accept for shipment any article whose greatest dimension exceeds 1 yard. What should I do?

Answer: Pack it diagonally in a cubical case 1 yard on a side. The length of the diagonal is $\sqrt{3} = 1.73^{+}$ yards.

Source not quoted as author gave the wrong answer

USEFUL HINTS IN WRITING LOVE LETTERS

The language of the gentleman's letters and the thoughts expressed in them throughout the entire period of courtship should be coloured with the most delicate shades of exalted sentiment and respect for that superior, intuitive refinement of woman, the richest heritage of her sex — which, weathering the storms of every civilization since the earliest dawn of human history, has been preserved, immutable and immaculate.

The gentleman should commence his letter: 'Dear Miss (surname)'. In time, as the correspondence develops greater freedom, the given name of the lady may be used, preceded by 'Dear Miss', and finally the 'Miss' may be dispensed with and the salutation 'Dear (given name)' used until the close of the courtship.

Such extravagant expressions as 'My own sweet darling', 'Dearest Ducky', 'Honey', 'Pet', etc, are in very bad taste, and when used by a bewhiskered man, old enough to vote, or by a matured woman, would suggest the presence of incipient dementia, rather than the ardent passion which they are supposed to portray.

In closing love letters be governed by the same condition referred to in the directions given for commencing the letter, using the following closings progressively: 'Yours respectfully', 'Yours very truly', 'Yours sincerely', 'Yours affectionately', 'Ever yours', 'Most affectionately yours', 'Ever yours affectionately', etc. Any variation of the above examples would be proper.

(continued on page 103)

The Marriage of Miss Anna Bloch and Mr Willis Dashwood, which was announced in this paper a few weeks ago, was a mistake and we wish to correct.

Colorado paper

GOOD HORSE, complete with saddle and bridle, 6 volt battery, pistons, connecting rods, etc.

Advert in *Nigerian Times*

Referee McKercher called two policemen to the scene, and while the three were in discussion another hurtled over their heads.

The Sunday Times

Our own Bishop has promised to take the chair. There will be a very strong platform to support him.

Diocesan Magazine

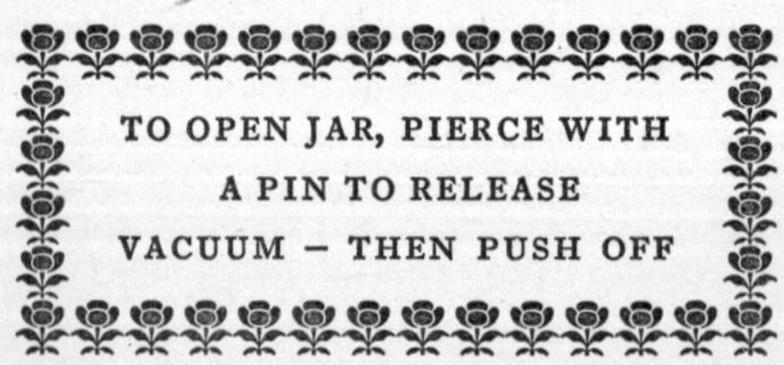

Inscription on fruit jar

Letter from Gentleman to Lady Asking Permission to Press His Suit

Dear Miss Gaither:

During the past year, which it has been my singular good fortune to be recognized favourably amongst your host of friends and admirers, I have been tempted, time and again, to confide to you a secret which lies nearest of all to my heart; but until now I have been restrained by an irrepressible doubt of my worthiness to aspire to so great a happiness as that which I now am about to ask at your hands.

Ever since I first had the honour and extreme pleasure of your acquaintance I have felt creeping upon me, with ever-growing force, signs of a sentiment far stronger than that of respectful regard and admiration.

If this frank avowal does not fail to meet with a disposition on your part, at least, to cultivate a responsive sentiment, should such not yet be the state of your feelings, will you do me the honour to recognize my suit and accept me as an ardent aspirant for your heart and hand?

Earnestly hoping for an early and favourable reply.

I am, respectfully yours,
SIGMUND GRANVILLE

Reply to above

Dear Mr Granville:

Your very kind letter of May 10th came to me in the nature of a surprise, but a pleasant one I must confess.

Our long and agreeable acquaintance certainly justifies you in claiming from me the warmest sentiment of esteem and respect, sentiments which often ripen into feelings of a more tender kind.

With the approval of my parents, who I have consulted, the request which you have made has been favourably considered, and it will afford me keen pleasure to accept the kind attentions which you propose.

Very sincerely yours,
MYRTLE GAITHER
From *Book of Love Letters*
by Joshua Whitcombe (Baltimore, 1912)

Just to let you know that your patient has been booked for her confinement under Miss Watson's car, on the recommendation of the Public Health Authority.

Letter received by a doctor

Miss Sandiston, who is only 19, has grown since last year. In patches her form is most impressive.

Essex paper

Walking sedately before the bride, came her small nephew George Stainer 3rd, carrying the ring and two little nieces of the groom.

Roswell (New Mexico) *Dispatch*

Southampton Flower Show was found by a mushroom picker in the Ettlingen Forest, near Karlsruhe, Germany. It had drifted 470 miles.

Yorkshire Evening Press

Owing to the disastrous fire, the Grange Hotel has temporarily moved to Greyfields Manor Hotel, where the welcome will be even warmer.

Advert in ABC railway timetable

SCIENTIFIC INFERENCE
by CHRISTOPHER S. O'D. SCOTT

You are given a large number of identical inscrutable boxes. You are to select one, the 'target box', by any means you wish which does not involve opening any boxes, and you then have to say something about what is in it. You may do this by any means you wish which does not involve opening the target box.

This apparent miracle can easily be performed. You only have to select the target box at random, and then open a random sample of other boxes. The contents of the sample boxes enable you to make an estimate of the contents of the target box which will be better than a chance guess. To take an extreme case, if none of the sample boxes contains a rabbit and your sample is large, you can state with considerable confidence: 'The target box does not contain a rabbit'. In saying this, you make no assumption whatever about the principles which may have been used in filling the boxes.

This process epitomizes scientific induction at its simplest, which is the basis of all scientific inference. It depends only on the existence of a method of randomizing – that is, on the assumption that events can be found which are unrelated (or almost) to given events.

It is usually thought that scientific inference depends upon nature being orderly. The above shows that a seemingly weaker condition will suffice: scientific inference depends upon our knowing ways in which nature is disorderly.

From *The Scientist Speculates* ed. I. J. Good
(Heinemann, 1962)

IVY CREEPS THROUGH WINDOW,
STRANGLES SEPTUAGENARIAN

Apocryphal headline

Lawrence Beal has recovered from a visit to relatives in Newcastle NH and Boston.

Ellsworth (Maine) *American*

Lady, having spent Christmas with her family, strongly recommends comfortable homely hotel.

Advert in Sussex paper

Two-room basement apartment, hot and cold water, shower in basement. Private entrance. Almost private bath.

Advert in *Lawrence* (Kansas) *Journal-World*

Four riders cleared the course of about 800 yards with 14 obstacles, including Miss Richardson (Britain) on Cobler.

Scottish Sunday Express

Birkenhead fire brigade were on the scene within a few minutes but by that time the fire had a good hold. Firemen were leaping up through the glass roof to a height of about 50 feet and streams of molten wax poured from the building.

Liverpool Evening Express

GIRL WANTED for petrol pump attendant.

Advert in *Oxford Mail*

'We've had a jolly time,' he continued. 'We get letters from home regularly and when we went to New York we saw the Aquarium. We were disappointed to find that the octopus had just died, but it was all right because the next day, what do you think? I met Mrs Roosevelt.'

Boston Traveler

WOMEN, the poets tell us, are nearest to the angels. I can confirm that statement.

Brunhilde van Druysen is 8 ft 6 ins high; Elsa van Druysen is merely 7 ft 4 ins high. Brunhilde weighs 365 lb; Elsa weighs 345 lb. Work that out.

I have been interviewing them. Cures for a crick in the neck can be addressed to me, care of this office. It happened at an afternoon rehearsal for Mr Bertram Mills's annual circus at Olympia, Kensington, where they are shortly to appear.

'Neither of us,' said Elsa, 'believes in the habit of slimming. We are not big eaters, but we like snacks frequently. For breakfast Brunhilde had 12 eggs and a pound of bacon; for lunch only two pounds of beefsteak and a couple of cauli-flowers, with a few chips. For tea – we love your English tea, but not your teacups – just a dozen or so of pastries and a loaf or two of bread.

'Dinner is our best meal, the one we really enjoy. We have ordered for this evening twelve pounds of fried fish each with fried potatos and more tea.'

Daily Mail, Dec. 21st, 1932

● It is possible to dry angleworms until they are only 46 per cent water, and still revive them, but they die if they become only one-fifth of 1 per cent drier than 46 per cent.

Binghampton (NY) *Press*

LOST

Antique cameo ring, depicting Adam
and Eve in Market Square Saturday
night.

> Advert in Essex paper

Owing to a printer's error in the 'Fairy-ring' cake recipe
last week 'two ounces castor oil' was given for 'two ounces
caster sugar'. We apologize for this silly mistake.

> *Reveille*

It was a hot day and the effect of cooked fish left standing
for an unknown time on the tummy of a homeward-bound
excursionist was not pleasant to contemplate.

> *Daily Mail*

We forwarded your enquiry re nettle tea to the writer of the
recipe in our issue of July 20th, but have received a notification
from his executors' solicitors to say that he is now deceased.

> Gardening paper

☞ NO GAMES ☜
KEEP BEACH CLEAR FOR LITTERS

> Notice at Silvermine Bay, Hongkong

Gobfrey Shrdlu has not been so much in evidence lately in the matter of misprints and grammatical errors; perhaps editors are becoming more careful. This means that the remainder of the items in this book are 'Funny Confusing', i.e. oddities and eccentricities.

A CASE OF DOUBLE MISRECOGNITION

About May, 1901, Mrs Piddington wrote to a friend, Miss Lilian Allen, of 2A Lower Grosvenor Place s w, inviting her to lunch. As she received no answer for several days, she went to call at Miss Allen's house. Miss L. Allen was not at home, but her sister, Miss Gertrude Allen was.

Mrs Piddington explained to Miss G. Allen that she had called to find out if Miss L. Allen was coming to lunch with her, as she had not written. Miss G. Allen said that her sister had met Mrs Piddington in the street and given her a verbal answer. Mrs Piddington denied this, and added that she had not seen Miss L. Allen for some months. Miss L. Allen then came in, and explained the mystery as follows:

'Some days ago meeting a lady in the street, whom I thought to be Mrs Piddington, I stopped in order to speak to her. The lady said she had written me a note asking me to lunch but she did not mention the day or hour. I accepted the invitation, and we then walked together along the street for some minutes, and the lady conversed with me about my sister, and said: "I've asked you and your sister". In reply to this remark I said that my sister could not go out to lunch. (Miss Gertrude Allen being in bad health rarely goes out.) The lady looked astonished, but we parted without further remark, I never doubting that I had been talking to Mrs Piddington. On my return home I found a note from Mrs Piddington asking me to lunch. As I thought I had just given her a verbal acceptance I did not send a written reply.

'This morning I met this same lady again. She stopped me and explained that she had mistaken me for some one else, and I then found out *my* mistake. She explained that she had written to ask two sisters to lunch; and when, after her conversation with me (whom she had mistaken for one of these two sisters), both sisters (I having refused on my sister's behalf) turned up, explanations ensued, and she discovered her mistake.'

The above was dictated to Mr Piddington partly by Miss L. Allen and partly by Mrs Piddington on August 1st, 1901, with the exception of a few alterations and additions made on May 12th, 1902, at Miss Allen's dictation.

Miss Allen states that her eyesight is normal, and that she now sees that there was a slight, but by no means a striking, resemblance between Mrs Piddington and the lady whom she mistook for her.

Miss Lilian Allen and Mrs Piddington were well known to each other at the time of this incident, but Miss Allen admits that she is prone to mistaking people by sight. She has not up to the present time (May, 1902) again seen the strange lady whom she mistook for Mrs Piddington. Another coincidence is that the strange lady spoke to Miss Lilian Allen of 'your sister Mabel', and that Miss Allen really has a sister Mabel.

The episode is instructive, because, had the mystery never been solved, as might well have happened, it would have contained all the elements of what might not unreasonably have been claimed as a case of veridical hallucination.

Journal of the Society for Psychical Research,
November, 1902

A **WOMAN READER** took Middlesbrough's *Evening Gazette* literally when editor Ian Fawcett invited election questions 'in a nutshell'.

She carefully prised the kernel out of a walnut, inserted her brief question, glued the nut down and posted it to the *Gazette*. The question was not, however, among those which were put to a panel of candidates in a local TV programme. The editor exercised his discretion as well as his nut-crackers.

'It was too nutty,' he said.

UK Press Gazette

George Parker Bidder (1806-78), the 'elder Bidder', was born at Moreton Hamstead, in Devonshire, where his father carried on a small business as a stone-mason. At the early age of four, Bidder showed a most extraordinary ability for calculation and was exhibited as a prodigy. Nevertheless, strange as it seems, at the age of six, he learned from an elder brother to count to 10 and then to 100. This was the only formal instruction in figures that he ever received . . .

Before long Bidder was taken about the country by his father for the purpose of exhibition. This was so profitable for the father that the boy's education was entirely neglected . . . The following series shows the increasing rapidity with which the answers came:

1816 (ten years of age): 'What is the compound interest on £4,444 for 4,444 days at 4 per cent per annum?' *Answer*, in 2 minutes, £2,434 16s 5¼d.

1817 (still ten years of age): 'How long would a cistern 1 mile cube be filling, if receiving from a river 120 gallons per minute, without intermission?' *Answer*, in 2 minutes, 14,300 years, 285 days, 12 hours, 46 minutes. (The reader may like to work out this sum to ascertain whether due account has been taken of leap-years!)

1818 (eleven years of age): 'Divide 468,592,413,563 by 9076.' *Answer*, within 1 minute, 51,629,838.

1818 (twelve years of age); 'If the pendulum of a clock vibrates the distance of 9¾ inches in a second of time, how many inches will it vibrate in 7 years, 14 days, 2 hours, 1 minute, 56 seconds, each year being 365 days, 5 hours, 48 minutes, 55 seconds?' *Answer*, in less than a minute, 2,165,625,744¾ inches.

1819 (thirteen years of age): 'Find the number whose cube less 19 multiplied by its cube shall be equal to the cube of 6.' *Answer*, instantly, 3.

From *Mental Prodigies* by Fred Barlow
(Hutchinson, 1951)

COMPLETE canary breeding outfit; oil drum, 2 five-gallon cans. 318 Earle Street, 3rd floor, after 5.

New Bedford (Mass.) *Standard-Times*

Mrs Carolynn Wilkin, 22-year-old wife of a Whitton gunmaker, has developed an unconventional art form – pictures based on spaghetti. She also employs other kinds of pasta and pasta circles, stars and wheels. 'The idea came to me at Christmas when I was trying to think of a way of giving inexpensive presents,' Mrs Wilkin explained. 'I'd never tried anything artistic before.'

Thames Valley Telegraph

A CIRCUS MAN in Bor, Yugoslavia, who has already eaten more than 22,500 razor blades, a ton of brassware, cutlery, nuts, bolts and assorted ironware, has now bought himself a bus – which he intends to eat within the next two years.

Sunday Mirror

ALTHOUGH written many years ago, *Lady Chatterley's Lover* has just been re-issued by Grove Press, and this fictional account of the day-by-day life of an English gamekeeper is still of considerable interest to outdoor-minded readers, as it contains many passages on pheasant raising, the apprehending of poachers, ways to control vermin, and other chores and duties of the professional gamekeeper.

Unfortunately, one is obliged to wade through many pages of extraneous material in order to discover and savour these sidelights on the management of a Midland shooting estate, and in this reviewer's opinion the book cannot take the place of J. R. Miller's *Practical Gamekeeper*.

Review in the American magazine *Field and Stream*

Mr Trumper replied: 'Anyone should have known it was an elephant's trunk. I curled it up and put it into a parcel marked "Perishable". I had it specially cooked in Rhodesia because I thought if I brought it in raw I might fall foul of the foot and mouth restrictions.'

Torquay Times

THE EDITORS of a national fortnightly publication in pidgin which is to be introduced in New Guinea have promised prospective readers that it will be printed on 'nambawan (number one) smoke paper'.

This is to assure the inhabitants, most of whom roll their own cigarettes, that their newspaper will not let them down.

The Guardian

An elephant was washed up yesterday on a beach at Widemouth Bay, near Bude, Cornwall. Police believe it was thrown overboard after it died while being transported.

Daily Express

AUNT LOCKED UP FOR 41 YEARS

Havana police said they detained a brother and sister yesterday on a charge of having kept their aunt locked up in a room for 41 years to get a share of a small family inheritance.

Police found the woman lying naked on an old bed in a rat infested room in a Havana house. She had been locked up in 1923 and had been kept alive with small amounts of food.

Sheffield Telegraph, 1964

APART FROM an isolated incident of violence in 1470 when the dean of the faculty of arts was shot at with bows and arrows, and if one glosses over the Jacobite demonstrations of 1715, the university has been singularly free of student unrest.

> From the Prospectus of the University of
> St Andrews

THE END OF PERPETUAL MOTION

Mr Gobert of Philadelphia, who lately advertised that he would take any bet from five to one hundred thousand dollars on the feasibility of Mr Redheffer's *discovery* of perpetual motion, was taken up for five thousand dollars, by Mr Jacob Perkins of Newburyport.

After making a series of experiments in vain, to construct a moving machine upon Mr Redheffer's *self moving* principle, he *discovered* to his infinite chagrin, that Mr Redheffer had in the meantime moved himself off, with 20,000 dollars in notes of hand given him by Mr Gobert for his valuable secret. We understand that Mr Gobert has acknowledged his bet forfeited, and is now in pursuit of Redheffer, who keeps himself in perpetual motion to elude him.

> *Weekly Register*, 1813

Ill effects of the cravat. Wearing the cravat too tightly tied, induces distressing, and frequently very constant pain of both the head and eyes. During exertion of the body, it would be well to loosen it; and also, when engaged in profound study, writing, reading, etc. The body ought, in retiring to rest, to be divested of all ligatures. Evils of great magnitude have arisen from a neglect of these precautions.

> *Knowledge*, 1837

Martin C—, aged 46, was said by a police officer at Clerkenwell, last week, to have walked along Randolph Road, Camden Town, 'absolutely nude' on Sunday afternoon, shouting: 'How about this?'

North London Press

Dear Tom,

I have had a baby son by a Canadian. Your mother doesn't mind, so hope you won't. He has bought you a new motor-bike and is sending you 50 cigs a week.

Your loving wife, Mary

Quoted in weekly journal

At 11.59 on November 14th, about 300 people will set off on a five-mile hike to the 762-ft summit of Ivinghoe Beacon, in Hertfordshire. They will carry with them aspidistras in pots, or objects and plants resembling aspidistras, to take part in the World Aspidistra Show. At the summit they will compete in a so-called nut-cracking contest which entails pushing a block of wood round a marked course with their heads in the pitch dark.

Evening Standard

A constable with a bandaged ear told the Clerkenwell, London, magistrate yesterday that when he made enquiries about a car in Southampton Row, wc, a man who sat in it bit his ear. The man would not let go, and his teeth had to be forcibly removed.

News of the World

Jilted girl hired a groom to go on with her wedding

Her bridegroom-to-be jilted her at the last moment, but Patricia H— still had the wedding day she had planned – as the bride of a stranger. She 'hired' him in the park, for a fee of £20, to stand in at a register office 19 months ago for Kenneth Macdonald, the man who called things off.

Miss H— came away from the ceremony with a marriage certificate showing them to be Mr and Mrs Kenneth Macdonald. And yesterday, when she asked for a nullity decree, she presented a London Divorce Court judge with 'his strangest case in 42 years'. Commented Judge Beresford: 'It's not every day you walk in a park and hear of a man willing to go through a marriage ceremony with you.' Said Counsel, Mr Walter Merrylees: 'He was willing to do it – but only for £20.'

Explained 29-year-old Miss H— at her mother's home in Long Road, Lewisham last night: 'The Monday after Kenneth Macdonald said he did not want to marry me I went for a walk in the park and met a man. I never asked him his name. I arranged to meet him on the steps of Lewisham register office next morning. I told him I had a licence in the name of Kenneth Macdonald.'

The following day Miss H— and her mother kept the date with the stranger. Ten minutes after the wedding, Mrs Helen H— handed over the £20 on the pavement. Mr Mystery shook hands and went his way. Miss H— went home with mother. She has never seen the stranger since. She still does not know his name. And she is keeping the secret of why she went on with the ceremony – 'It is too personal,' she said. Judge Beresford granted Miss H—, who went to court as Mrs Macdonald, a nullity decree because the 'marriage' was legally void.

Daily Express

Another delightful touch was provided by the manufacturer of a new style of 'one-armed bandit' machine. His True Blue model, as supplied to golf clubs and Conservative clubs, had a picture of the Houses of Parliament on the front. For Working Men's clubs a scene of the British Legion marching past the Cenotaph was thought more suitable.

The Observer quoted in
New Statesman's 'This England' column

A man in Rio de Janeiro told the police someone had stolen from his home a lion's skin worth one hundred pounds. It had a great sentimental value for him, he said, because the lion, when alive and still in possession of its skin, 'ate a very good friend of mine who was with me on a hunting expedition'.

Reveille

It is strictly forbidden on our
Black Forest camping site that
people of different sex, for
instance, men and women, live
together in one tent unless they
are married with each other for
that.
The meaning of this regulation
is that otherwise the purpose of
the furlough, namely recreation,
could not be guaranteed.

Notice quoted in Caravan Club magazine

ROBERT BARKER was caught with more than his trousers down when the policeman came along. He had everything off … And yesterday the Portsmouth magistrates heard about the night he was found shivering in a dark alley.

'He had been trying to get into the supermarket next door but he couldn't squeeze through the skylight,' said Mr David Roebuck, prosecuting. 'He thought he would be able to get in if he took his clothes off – and that's just what he did. He pushed his clothes through the skylight, intending to follow after them, but, to his dismay, he still couldn't get in.'

Mr Roebuck said that 34-year-old Barker told PC Michael Sibley: 'Get me out of here, I'm frozen.' Barker, of Bolton Road, Portsmouth, pleaded guilty to entering the Fina Fare supermarket in Albert Road, Portsmouth, with intent to steal. He was fined £10, with £3 costs. Afterwards Barker, who is 5 ft 8 ins and weighs 10 stone, said: 'I had to shout to the policeman for help. What else could I do? It was daft, but I'd been drinking a bit.'

Daily Mail

Dear Dr James,

Patient No. T46001. Mr D. L. P—

This young man's sputum specimen has been examined and found entirely normal, but the carton in addition contained a bus ticket and a five pound note. I am still speculating as to how these can have got there but I have told him to come and fetch the five pound note.

Letter to doctor from laboratory

When asked why he was carrying a heavy iron gate hinge early in the morning at the premises of Messrs James, Croydon, Thompson was alleged to have replied, 'I was going to make a bird-cage'.

Sutton Times

WILSON'S POSER

'What I said is quite right,' said Wilson, 'Parker called out to my uncle to do something or other, when my nephew—'

'There you are again, Wilson. Once for all, are we to understand that both your uncle and your nephew were on the machine?'

'Certainly. I thought I made that clear. My nephew turned to Parker and said the engine wasn't running well, so Parker called out to my uncle—'

'Phew! I'm sorry to interrupt you again, Wilson, but we can't get on like this. Is it true that the flying-machine would only carry two?'

'Of course. I said at the start that it only carried two.'

'Then what do you mean by saying there were three persons on board?'

'Who said there were three?'

'Of course, Wilson, you meant us to understand that Parker is your uncle or your nephew.'

'He is no relation to me whatever. It's curious,' said Mr Wilson very deliberately, 'and it's rather sad how thickheaded some people are. You don't seem to grip the facts. It never seems to have occurred to you that my uncle and my nephew are one and the same man. Yes; David George Linklater is my uncle, and he is also my nephew. Consequently I am both his uncle and nephew. Queer, isn't it? I'll explain how it comes about.'

Mr Wilson put the case so very simply that his friends saw how it might happen without any marriage within the prohibited degrees. Perhaps the reader can work it out for himself.

Adapted from No 56 in H. E. Dudeney's
Amusements in Mathematics

SOLUTION. *If there are two men each of whom marries the mother of the other, and there is a son of each marriage, then each of such sons will be at the same time uncle and nephew of the other. There are other ways in which the relationship may be brought about, but this is the simplest.*

Technical Glossary

(Translation)

Three of the samples were chosen for detailed study.	The results on the others didn't make sense and were ignored.
These results will be reported at a later date.	I might possibly get round to this sometime.
Typical results are shown.	The best results are shown.
Although some detail has been lost in reproduction, it is clear from the original micrograph that …	It is impossible to tell from the micrograph.
The most reliable values are those of Jones.	He was a student of mine.
It might be argued that …	I have such a good answer to this objection that I shall now raise it.
Correct within an order of magnitude.	Wrong.
… accidentally strained during mounting.	… dropped on the floor.
… handled with extreme care throughout the experiments.	… not dropped on the floor.
It is clear that much additional work will be required before a complete understanding …	I don't understand it.
It is hoped that this work will stimulate further work in the field.	This paper isn't very good, but neither is any of the others on this miserable subject.
The agreement with the predicted curve is excellent.	Fair
… good	Poor
… satisfactory	Doubtful
… fair	Imaginary.

From *Metal Progress* and *Shipbuilding and Shipping Record*, quoted in *The Scientist Speculates*, ed. I. J. Good

DECORATOR KILLED BY SCISSORS

A man was accidentally stabbed to death yesterday while paperhanging at his home at Ockbrook, near Derby. Mr Sidney Ashton, aged 65, fell from a plank supported by trestles and a pair of scissors he was carrying in his decorator's apron pierced his stomach. A doctor called to his home found him dead.

The Times

A Jolly Book for Jolly Folks
15 stamps
All about Girls and their Doings
Girls who want money – Big Girls at School – Big Girls at Home – Breach of Promise Girls – Novel Reading Girls – Girls with Sweethearts – Girls who are Fast – Girls who are Wicked – Girls who cost Money – Sensible Girls – Silly Girls – Girls who can spend Money – Girls of the Period – Girls who are Mothers – My Girl – Dirty Girls – Music Hall Girls – Jealous Girls – Carrotty Girls – Buxom Girls – Old Girls – Marrying Girls.

Profusely illustrated – coloured plates.

Advert in *The Novelty*, 1882

SECRETS
OF
SUCCESS

Or, the MONEY MAKER'S GUIDE – How to start a successful business. How Publicans, Jewellers, Tobacconists, etc., may greatly improve their business. How cheats victimize the unwary. How to engage the affections, without regard to wealth, age, or beauty. How to cure indigestion, nervousness and headaches. How to transform a pale and sallow face into one of health and beauty. How to make people loathe and detest the very thought of intoxicating drinks. Together with 200 Modern Ways of Making Money Honestly. Price 1*s*, post free. 13 stamps.

Advert in *The Novelty* 1882

On December 30th, 1793, died at Beaumaris, William Lewis, Esq, of Llandisman, in the act of drinking a cup of Welsh ale, containing about a wine quart, called a *tumbler maur*. He made it a rule, every morning of his life, to read so many chapters in the Bible, and in the evening, as a digestion of his morning study, to drink full eight gallons of ale. It is calculated that in his lifetime he must have drunk a sufficient quantity to float a seventy-four gun ship.

His size was astonishing: it is supposed that the diameter of his body was no less than two yards. He weighed forty stone. He died in his parlour; a lucky circumstance, as it would have been impossible to have got him down stairs; as it was, it was found necessary to have a machine, in form of a crane, to lift him on a carriage, and afterwards to have the same brought in to the church-yard to let him down into his grave. He went by the name of the King of Spain and his family by the different titles of Prince, Infanta, etc., but from what circumstance we know not.

The Cabinet of Curiosities, 1831

This is the story of four men and a woman, spanning the years from the height of the war to the present day. It takes in an underwear hunt.

Hertfordshire, Hemel Hempstead Gazette

GRAVE DECISION

When Robert Lee Terrell applied for his security benefits in 1963 in Macon, Georgia, he was unable to give his age when asked. Told to bring proof, he returned with his mother's gravestone which showed that, as she died in 1901, he was at least 62 years old and was entitled to benefits.

Reveille

'Fortunately we're insured against Acts of God,' said the Vicar after lightning struck, sending rafters crashing down on the church altar.

Acton Gazette

Bulmer, in his *Artificial Changeling*, speaks of a common soldier, who, in his presence, ate nothing but stones for twenty-four hours together; adding, that he is said sometimes to have ate half a peck of stones in a day.

Another Lithophagus, or stone-eater, was brought to Avignon, May 1760, who not only swallowed flints of an inch and a half long, a full inch broad, and half an inch thick, but such stones as he could reduce to powder, as marbles, pebbles, etc., he made up into paste, 'which to him was a most agreeable and wholesome food'. He swallowed flints about twenty-five a day, one day with another.

He was blooded, at Paris, by some physicians, and, in two hours, his blood became as fragile as coral. This last account was taken by Grainger (see his Biographical History) from Father Paulian's Dictionnaire Physique. – We ourselves remember a foreigner eating a plate-full of stones, at the Royal Circus in St. George's Fields, and afterwards (to do away all doubt) opening his waistcoat, and walking to the boxes, where the spectators knocked at his abdomen, when the desired rattling of the swallowed pebbles was heard by the wondering audience with delight ineffable.

The Cabinet of Curiosities, 1831

MACHINE-SHUCKED SHELLFISH

The US Bureau of Commercial Fisheries has devised a machine that can remove the edible part of shellfish and discard the shell. In a restaurant you expect to be presented with fresh shellfish that you can eat straight from the shell, but if shellfish are to reach the widest market they must be offered in tins and frozen. This means that they must first be shelled and cleaned. Unfortunately this is a labour-intensive activity that could cost a lot less if it were automated.

The scallop shucking machine washes the shellfish before blasting them with an oxy-acetylene torch to open them up. The top shell is removed and the inside washed before a second oxy-acetylene torch makes the mussel let go of its shell.

World Fishing quoted in *New Scientist*

Two student members of the Oxford University Railway Society, Mr A. P. Brereton and a friend, recently decided to emulate or better the performance of two London University students who, in 1959, travelled over all the, then, electrified lines of London Transport in a working day. The Oxford contenders had a rather tough task before them as the electrified lines now include the Rickmansworth–Amersham line and the Chalfont & Latimer to Chesham branch.

Only July 28th, armed with 'Twin-Rover' tickets and using public transport only, they started at 5.14 AM from Ongar, on the Central Line, and finished at Upminster precisely at midnight. As the attempt was made on a Saturday, they were unable to travel to Aldwych, but the Waterloo & City line (which takes five times as long to travel over) was included for good measure. The Olympia branch was omitted from the itinerary by both parties.

The 1959 champions covered 315 miles in 19 hrs 15 mins, but the 1962 contenders, by a more efficient itinerary covered 303, excluding the Amersham and Chesham runs. The total time taken by the Oxford pair, including the runs over the last two lines mentioned, was 18 hrs 46 mins, and, by so doing, another record has been set up in this era of records. Average speed in both cases was 16 miles an hour.

Railway Magazine, October 1962

A man who shot himself in the arm to drain snake poison from his blood stream was fined £2 at Taree, Australia – for carrying a firearm on a Sunday.

Charles Peters, of Coolongalook, was bitten while lying near a log. As he had no knife, he held his rifle to his arm and shot himself to make the bite bleed. He tied string around his arm as a tourniquet before he fainted.

Peters was found by hikers and taken to hospital where he was interviewed the same day by a detective – and later charged.

Weekly paper

PIG OF THE POPS

The music master of Louis XI of France, Abbé Debaigne, devised a very unusual instrument. He selected a dozen pigs whose squeals had a different pitch and arranged them in musical scale order.

He then made a keyboard, connecting the appropriate keys by sharp-pointed wires to the backs of the pigs. When the keys were depressed the pigs were pricked. They squealed and so produced some semblance of a tune.

Weekly paper

A RUNAWAY COW LANDS ON
A GREENHOUSE ROOF

Headline in Daily Mirror

AUSTRIAN/GERMAN/SWISS CHEFS
required for new French Restaurants

Evening News

If horseshoes bring good luck, blacksmith George Flinders must be a very lucky man indeed. He has the biggest stack of horseshoes in the world. At his smithy in the Nottinghamshire village of Scarrington, Mr Flinders began the stack in June 1945. From then onwards he began piling up used horseshoes – all interlocked neatly as he removed them from the horses' hooves.

Today it has grown to 17 feet in height, with a weight of more than 10 tons. Mr Flinders has calculated that there are 50,000 shoes in the stack. He has collected £65 for the local church funds by selling sixpenny postcards of his 'good luck' pile to tourists.

Reveille

Police who arrested two men on car-theft charges in New York said they belonged to a gang who offered their customers a guarantee. They sold stolen Cadillacs on the understanding that they were in sound mechanical condition. But if a defect developed the gang guaranteed to re-steal the car so that the illegal owner could claim its full value from his insurance company – usually about four times what he had paid for it.

Weekend

'Defector' wanted to watch girls

From Our Own Correspondent, New York, Feb. 8

A Yugoslav seaman was stranded in Connecticut today, the reluctant recipient of 'political asylum' which he did not really want.

Mr Siatko Sili, aged 31, a greaser on a Liberian tanker, 'defected' quite accidentally from his ship at the weekend when he decided to indulge in the innocent pleasure of watching some American girls.

To this purpose he called at the Brass Rail bar in New London and uttered the only English word he knew: 'Immigration'. It set off a chain reaction of confusion which spiralled up through the United States Immigration Service, the State Department, a Senator's office and finally into the White House Situations Room.

As a result Mr Sili was granted what amounted to temporary asylum and taken into custody by American officials. He was still there when his ship sailed.

The Times (by permission)

Denys Parsons
Funny Funny Funny 40p

A wonderful new volume of amusing, amazing, confusing
and convulsing misprints, howlers and oddities. On the
left-hand pages are the Funny Ha Ha items and on the right-
hand pages the Funny Peculiar pieces. Together they provide
hours of hilarity and mirth.

Funny Ha Ha and Funny Peculiar 35p

Denys Parsons' first superb collection of clangers and items
of rare fascination – all taken from newspapers and other
published sources.

Funny Ho Ho and Funny Fantastic 35p

For your further enjoyment here is another collection of
howlers and misprints.

Funny Amusing and Funny Amazing 35p

A side-splitting companion to the impartial, impenitent
and occasionally improper collections of Denys Parsons.